What Other.

"I'm grateful that Stephen De Silva has finally put prosperity in the proper light: by defining it by the condition of your soul, not your wallet."

—**Dave Ramsey**, host, *The Dave Ramsey Show*; bestselling author, *The Total Money Makeover*

"There are two fatal and opposite errors that rob us of happiness and pull us off the path of a prosperous soul. Steve illuminates these errors and teaches how to avoid their grip."

—**Verne Harnish**, CEO, Gazelles; author, *Mastering the Rockefeller Habits*

"Steve De Silva is a fresh, challenging and encouraging author. *Money and the Prosperous Soul* is a financial book based on the remarkable prayer from 3 John 1:2 'that you would prosper and be in health, even as your soul prospers.' Although God does not promise to make us rich, He clearly uses money to test our faithfulness and help us achieve that which is ultimately most significant. This book guides readers through their own journey toward a prosperous soul."

—**Howard Dayton**, founder, Compass—Finances God's Way; co-founder, Crown Financial Ministries

"A tool that can impart wisdom and unveil a purpose to enlist millions of believers into becoming active participants in the great transfer of wealth spoken of in the Bible. My heart leaped as, page after page, Steve took me beyond my high expectations into realms I could only imagine. A masterpiece that could equip a generation to succeed where others have failed."

—from the foreword by **Bill Johnson**, senior leader, Bethel Church (Redding, CA); author, *When Heaven Invades Earth* and *Face to Face with God*

"Thank you, Steve, for tunneling deep on the subject of wealth. You dig up a gold mine of unique insights because you have done the hard work to forge a gold mind, illuminated by the Spirit. By challenging each of us to come to terms with faulty thinking on this subject, you create a fresh place for us to discover our individual purpose and sphere of influence. Your book shows us how it is possible to fill that sphere with the supernatural provision needed. If we all do what you teach, Jesus will be seen as the answer to the desire of nations. A brilliant book!"

—**Lance Wallnau**, Lance Learning Group

"I met Steve thirteen years ago when he offered his CPA experience free of charge to our fledgling church as a blessing. A successful CPA, pastor, teacher and now author, Steve brings his years of practical experience together and offers a clear, helpful path in understanding God's call to each of us as stewards of His resources. Steve's insights will give many a useful handle in the everyday events of spiritual formation into Christlikeness. His wisdom and no-nonsense approach to the naturally supernatural aspects of how we steward all that God entrusts to us will leave you humbled, encouraged, convicted and equipped for change."

—**Mike Kerns**, senior pastor, Vineyard Church of Redding; co-founder and CEO, YAKS Koffee Shops; president, Forever Love International

"Bookshelves today creak under the weight of myriad books written on the subject of finance. Add to that the vicissitudes of our times, and we find it even more difficult to navigate a balance between experiencing personal prosperity and honoring God. Steve has written with clarity and practicality, revealing that knowing how to do the math, coupled with experiencing the miraculous, is the equation for Kingdom solvency. I encourage you to ponder every principle with the confidence that you are reading more than mere theory. You are reading truth that has been put on trial and proven reliable."

—**Randall Worley**, Ph.D.

"'Red sky at night, sailor's delight.' Prepare to take a voyage that will lead you to God's true riches in your life."

—**Rick Sbrocca**, CEO, Spiritus Solutions, LLC

"Author Steve De Silva has hit a home run. In the past thirty years I have started seven companies, including a marketplace consulting business. Over these years I have observed scores of people struggling with serious financial issues without any real resolution. They finally wind up getting financial counseling from someone, or reading some book that teaches them various budgeting skills but never really deals with the root issues of their hearts. Soon after, they find themselves in the same bondage all over again.

"Years ago I heard someone say, 'If you need money, don't ask for money; ask why you need money.' Like an experienced heart surgeon, Steve unearths the very core issues of our lives that perpetuate poverty and undermine wealth. This book is not another of those get-rich-quick schemes but a life voyage though the seas of adversity to the shores of prosperity. *Money and the Prosperous Soul* is a must-read for everyone who wants to live in peace and leave a legacy."

—**Kris Vallotton**, senior associate leader, Bethel Church (Redding, CA); co-founder, Bethel School of Supernatural Ministry; author, *The Supernatural Ways of Royalty* and *Purity, the New Moral Revolution*

"With this book Stephen De Silva has bridged the gap between the spiritual and the marketplace. Our company's guiding principle— "Living in His presence, resting in His provision, demonstrating His Kingdom"—requires a marriage of Kingdom principles to Kingdom power. Thanks to Stephen's wisdom, I now have a stronger grasp of Kingdom principles and how our business can demonstrate Kingdom power more fully on a daily basis. His insights into our need for developing a prosperous soul in order to see the Kingdom of God come with power have, for me, been personally transformative and, I believe, will soon be for our company as well."

—**Doug Hignell**, CEO, The Hignell Companies; Ph.D., Stanford Graduate School of Business

"Stephen's Prosperous Soul workshop set me free to prosper, and I am pleased to see that his book carries the same anointing. Rather than a how-to book on steps to financial prosperity, he challenges your beliefs about money and reveals God's boundless love available to you. He offers freedom from the inner chains that bind you to a 'less than' mentality so that you, too, can become a prosperous soul, living in the abundance of the Kingdom—both seen and yet to come."

—**Julia Loren**, author, *When God Says Yes: His Promise and Provision When You Need It Most*

"*Money and the Prosperous Soul* is an exceptional book rich with divine inspiration. Every page is loaded with truth and overflows with a wealth of godly wisdom. Steve's remarkable journey portrays this reality, and his proven character serves as a roadmap for those desiring to live a prosperous life. I am delighted to introduce a book that is thoughtful, authentic and, most of all, extremely practical."

—**Larry Randolph**, conference speaker; author,
User Friendly Prophecy

"My friend Steve has crafted into remarkably few pages an expansive and profound understanding and application of living in the abundance of God's Kingdom. No armchair quarterbacking here, as Steve expounds with the authority of one who knows from practice that the core value is relational—an inner life of passionate pursuit of Father God and His eyes, heart and values in which true riches serve people and not the other way around. Steve guides us in how to avoid the traps of Mammon, Poverty spirit, debt, consumerism and materialism. The key? Finding your divine purpose, 'which is in you as grain is in wood,' and we uncover it in direct and intimate fellowship with Him. The sections on the fruit of the Sabbath, toil versus work and plans versus purpose are alone worth the price of the book. A stunning volume."

—**André Van Mol**, M.D., family physician; vice president,
PrayNorthState; board member, Moral Revolution

"Steve's writing is filled with prophetic and practical hope, provoking our hearts to a well-balanced paradigm shift from today's prevailing hopelessness and despair, following models of fear (spirit of Poverty) and greed (spirit of Mammon), to restoring our ultimate hope in our purpose and identity in God. I recommend Steve's book to all who want to be entrusted with the true riches of the Kingdom, who choose to have a hopeful perspective, God's perspective—the true revelation of hope and the wisdom of a Joseph."

—**Bob Hartley**, founder and president, the Hartley Institute

MONEY AND THE PROSPEROUS SOUL

Tipping the Scales of Favor and Blessing

STEPHEN K. DE SILVA

Chosen

a division of Baker Publishing Group
Grand Rapids, Michigan

Published by Chosen Books
a division of Baker Publishing Group
P.O. Box 6287, Grand Rapids, MI 49516-6287
www.chosenbooks.com

Printed in the United States of America

Library of Congress Cataloging-in-Publication Data
De Silva, Stephen K., 1961–
    Money and the prosperous soul : tipping the scales of favor and blessing / Stephen K. De Silva.
       p. cm.
    Includes bibliographical references.
    ISBN 978-0-8007-9496-5 (pbk.)
    1. Christian stewardship—Pentecostal churches. 2. Money—Religious aspects—Pentecostal churches. I. Title.
BV772.D42 2010
248'.6—dc22
                                      2010014603

11   12   13   14   15   16   7   6   5   4   3

To those fierce enough not to settle.

Contents

Foreword

When I picked up this manuscript, I was excited for my friend and co-worker Steve De Silva. He had finished his book, which I knew to be an important goal in his life. Steve has taught this subject faithfully to our church family and managed the economics of the Bethel Church ministry the entire time I have served as its senior leader.

Little did I know, however, that in picking up this manuscript, I would have the sense that I was holding in my hands a tool that could impart wisdom and unveil a purpose to enlist millions of believers into becoming active participants in the great transfer of wealth spoken of in the Bible. My heart leaped as, page after page, Steve took me beyond my high expectations into realms I could only imagine.

Steve De Silva has a masterpiece with *Money and the Prosperous Soul*—one that could equip a generation to succeed where others have failed.

Books on money are common. Each fills a vital role. But this one prophesies, preparing us for a mission beyond the obvious mandates given in sermon after sermon. On these pages you will commence a journey of divine purpose far greater than most of us have ever imagined. This book is about shaping the course of history by getting healthy on the inside, and then living from the inside out. Once Kingdom health is experienced on the inside of the believer, it is to be exported to shape the world around us—thus the phrase *prosperous soul*.

The common themes of contentment, generosity and living without debt are here, as they should be. Steve gives us tools to live counter to the devastating norms surrounding us. Someone wisely said that "vision gives pain a purpose." If there is pain involved in shifting from serving Mammon to being an authentic steward of Kingdom finances, it is far overshadowed by the joyful vision of transformed cities and nations through a people who have discovered what it is to live with a last-days stewardship mandate.

While I have enjoyed almost every book on finances I have ever read, one thing has always been missing for me: the supernatural. When the supernatural is discussed in the context of money, fear often spreads through the camp as we recall story after story of abuse from ministries and individuals who used the "God factor" as the excuse for financial carelessness, hoping God would bail them out. Yet overreaction to error usually leads to more error.

While we have seen devastation caused to families and churches, history also contains the record of supernatural supply with divine purpose. The Bible is filled with stories of success *because* of the supernatural without yielding to a "lottery" mentality. In other words, it can be done right. That is the most unique part of *Money and the Prosperous Soul*. Steve revels in the role of the supernatural in the believer's world of economics without abandoning the wisdom gained on the subject through his years of training and Bible study.

This book is practical yet visionary. It is structured in all the right ways, yet is intensely prophetic. Steve takes a healthy approach to this subject that should excite and ignite almost every reader.

Welcome to the journey of a lifetime!

Bill Johnson
Senior leader, Bethel Church, Redding, California
Author, *When Heaven Invades Earth* and
Face to Face with God

Introduction

The Voyage

We can find ourselves in a good book. Stories can spark perspective, hope and victory in a person's life. My prayer for you is that the following pages would spark the journey of your own prosperous soul. To that end, imagine you are on a voyage.

You are the captain of a cargo ship, responsible to acquire, protect, manage and deliver merchandise for its rightful owners—you are a steward. In spite of your skills as a sailor, you have suffered loss from time to time. Foul weather has required you to jettison cargo, doldrums have threatened, but you have sailed on through tempests and calm. This is your profession; you are a dealer and transporter of goods from port to port.

Then one day you receive a great commission—a voyage that will require you to sail far beyond the familiar harbors and stretches of ocean. The risks are great, but the reward is greater. The one who has chartered your ship is the most successful merchant in the world. He is looking for business partners, and this voyage is to be the first stage leading to a permanent partnership. When he approaches, you are skeptical that your small-time cargo ship could be a viable candidate for his fleet. But he quickly explains that your craft will be refitted at many of the ports on the journey in order to accommodate the accumulating goods. Your task is to deliver these goods at a final destination on a faraway shore. It is the opportunity of a lifetime, so you accept.

The next day you weigh anchor and set sail for open seas. You look out and see the jagged contours of the mountainous islands that have long stood tall and menacing at the borders of your usual trade routes. Concealed rocks and shallows around these islands have wrecked many a ship and often damaged your own. Strange currents have swept some vessels in eddying circles for months and years. But though these islands are notorious for their dangers, you and your crew have sailed here for generations. You've become comfortable in these familiar waters.

You study a map provided by the merchant. It reveals a different perspective on the dangerous chain of islands; they are marked with a simple word: *Poverty*. The map reveals that these islands obstruct your course. You must first navigate past them and leave them behind for unknown waters. Thus, your first new challenge is simply to abandon routine, which isn't easy. As dangerous as these islands have been, at least they were *familiar*. You felt confident sailing around them, even when they threatened destruction.

Gradually, your courage rises and you sail on, stretching the distance between your ship and those perilous shores. The mountains melt in your wake, leaving you alone in a vast ocean with only a strange map and one dim hope.

Far ahead a new land appears. Pulling out the map, you notice there are more details than before—the map is expanding as your voyage progresses. Not only do you see a new string of islands, but the map reveals their name: *Mammon.* You realize that although these two island chains are beyond each other's sight, they fashion a corridor between which you must navigate. The map becomes vital, stressing unconventional course settings and highlighting menacing threats. Negotiating every new hazard—each distinct but all potentially disastrous to your voyage—constantly requires you to abandon your old trusted methods and learn new ones.

You continue to fix your course upon the merchant's destination and learn to trust the map, which always brings you safely to each port along the way. Just as the merchant had promised, there are outfitters at every port to restore and refit your ship, expanding its capacity and strength. Gradually, off in the distance, a faint shape forms on the horizon. Looking to the map, you catch your breath. A new country has emerged on the page. It is a vast continent, deep with promise, which the map simply names: *Destiny.*

Poverty and Mammon are spiritual influences that we all must learn to resist. Each of these spirits, like the islands in the voyage, has its own current, pulling upon our internal wounds and fears like magnets. And each features a host of pitfalls, both literal and spiritual, that are disastrous to wealth. Some believers perceive these influences as normal or unavoidable parts of everyday life—let's call them *familiar spirits*—and unintentionally allow their destructive effects into their lives. Other believers overcompensate in their avoidance of one spirit, putting themselves at risk of falling under the power of the other. We must continually consult the Holy Spirit for guidance and allow Him to train our vision upon our ultimate goal—Jesus, the One who has gone before us as our model of stewardship and the embodiment of the prosperous soul.

Where, you might ask, does a prosperous soul feature in this voyage story? It is the ship itself, where the condition of our souls is like the capacity of a ship. It determines what we can be entrusted to carry. Just as the islands threaten the ship, the dangers of Poverty and Mammon are targeted primarily at diminishing our soul's capacity, not merely our material possessions and circumstances. But the One who calls us to this journey does the opposite, growing our ability to carry wealth, both natural and spiritual. Our cooperation with God causes our souls to expand, according to John's prayer, even as our *soul prospers* (see 3 John 2).

1

Purpose

Where Is the Power?

The counselor's hat has a way of slipping onto the heads of various professionals who didn't ask for it. You know the classic scenario at the doctor's office: The patient starts rattling off all his physical problems, and before long he's baring his soul about his marriage, challenges at work and other stresses in his life. After all, he reasons, they are all connected. And so the doctor often becomes a counselor.

A similar fate pursues the accountant. Like a physical examination, accounting exposes the truth of people's personal affairs and, all too often, the need for some good advice to put those affairs in order. In my case, financial counseling came with the territory when I began my career as a certified public accountant in the mid-1980s. As a Christian, I wanted to marry my faith with my vocation, so for insight into money management I studied the Bible as well as the leading Christian financial teachers of the day: Larry Burkett,

Howard Dayton and Ron Blue to name a few. Armed with a harvest of revelation and information, I was confident that those I counseled were getting the soundest financial advice available.

As the years went by, however, I grew discouraged. The friends I counseled, though they began enthusiastically enough, seemed to find very little lasting breakthrough in changing their lifestyles. I knew that aligning their lives with biblical principles required them to swim against not only the tide of their own habits but also the current of prevailing messages in our culture. The hard part for them was admitting that, by all appearances, those cultural forces were winning. Though I was still convinced the wisdom and principles of Scripture were true, the message of biblical stewardship seemed to have merit without transforming power. Frankly, I was having the same experience and eventually concluded that having good financial understanding alone could not enable a believer to overcome financial struggles. Finally, I resigned myself to participating in a culture obsessed with affluence and impulse, and surrendered my counseling and teaching altogether—or so I thought.

In the years that followed, the Holy Spirit patiently continued His gentle work in the deepest waters of my heart. Gradually, I came to recognize the underlying root of my discouragement: The world's oppressions seemed more real than the promises of God. My heart resonated with Gideon's cry, "Where are all His miracles which our fathers told us about?" (see Judges 6:13). This problem fed an unresolved dissonance in my life, and I came to recognize it as injustice. Though I was willing to grimly bully my way forward with self-discipline, I found little joy and peace in this assignment, and it only served to underline my sense of injustice. When my experiences were measured against Christ's promise of "life more abundant," they fell pitifully short. It seemed that God had two conflicting goals for His followers: We were promised power and abundance, but apparently could only have them according to our own strength of self-discipline and acquisition. Our hearts thrilled to the idea of prosperity and fullness—abundance—yet it seemed the "spiritual" thing was to always be in the struggle against lack or excess. It was hard to find where the "abundant life" was in the midst of it all.

Enter: A Miracle

Bethel Church of Redding, California, is a place where *normal Christianity* implies the invading reality of heaven: "Thy Kingdom come." The church leadership team at Bethel is committed to living on the edge of faith, making room for the miraculous and never giving in to fear. When I joined the team as the chief financial officer, I was hungry to participate in this, but I repeatedly found myself stumbling upon a great chasm lying between my heavenly wishes and practical observations. It soon became apparent that God was either playing a cruel joke on me or strategically positioning me to experience breakthrough.

A church that lives on the edge of faith tends to have more than its share of storms and difficulties. I discovered that the reason we had so many testimonies of supernatural breakthrough around Bethel was that an entire company of people had decided to step regularly into difficult, even impossible, situations where only God could bring an answer. In particular, our leadership team had committed to practicing a level of radical financial generosity that constantly challenged what we perceived to be possible on paper. As the one handling that paper, I was the one most directly confronted by the contradiction between our desire to walk in the great promises of the Lord and the stark physical reality that made that walk nothing less than impossible. My old sense of injustice returned to question many of God's promises, until I saw that somehow the storm clouds always broke and we were still afloat. I began to learn a spiritual lesson: True faith in God lies in tension. Whether we are learning to die in order to live (see John 12:24) or scattering to increase all the more (see Proverbs 11:24), trusting Him requires us to live confidently between the problem and the promise—to live within a mystery (see 1 Corinthians 4:1).

A defining moment came in April of 2000. I found myself in a situation where I simply did not know what to do. It was a Wednesday, and our missionary and tithe commitments were due. We had $10,000, which was just enough to cover those bills. The problem lay in the coming Friday: payday. We needed $30,000 more if we were going to pay our employees.

The checkbook lay open on the floor before me. I walked in circles, praying aloud and explaining to God: *This is not a drill. I really need a miracle right now! Please provide the money.* In case He had forgotten, I reminded God of James 5:16: "The effective prayer of a righteous man can accomplish much." *I'm righteous by Your blood, and this is as fervent as I know how to get.* I admitted that I didn't know how this faith thing worked. Faced with what I felt could be an imminent disaster, all I could think to do was to continue walking in circles and petitioning.

Finally, I asked our senior pastor what to do. He suggested that we pray. "It has come to that!" he joked. I smiled unenthusiastically and gave a meager courtesy laugh. After we prayed, he directed me to pay the tithe and the missionaries. "We'll pray in the rest," he said. "God may still provide somehow."

"Shouldn't I use what we have to cover some of the payroll? These people have entrusted their livelihood to us. I feel responsible for them."

He pointed out that the same was true of the missionaries, and their due date was upon us now. We would take care of our immediate commitments and seek God for the rest. I did as he instructed, keenly aware that we had entered a moment of truth. Would God provide in time?

I whined, moaned, imagined the worst and continued to pour out my desperation in prayer. When I was spent, I wandered back to my office and collapsed in my chair, too distracted to work on anything else. Suddenly my telephone buzzed—someone had come to see me. "Send him in," I said.

A church member walked in, stood before me, smiled and handed me a check for $35,000. He told me he had been trying to deliver this gift for three months. "Problems kept coming up and cash flow struggles held it back. But today, here it is. I hope you can use it. See you later." With that, he stepped out of my office and into my heart's hall of fame.

Lifting my jaw off the floor, I sat and wept at God's deliverance. The check exactly matched the payroll, plus payroll tax deposits, needed the next day.

This provision had come in *after* we had made our payment of $10,000 to the missionaries and tithes. But what struck me most profoundly was that, while my prayers had been passionate during the crisis, God had established our deliverance three months prior, before I even knew of the need. I had acted as if I needed to get God's attention and convince Him to care about our necessities, when the reality was that God knew and cared far more about them than I.

I have never before or since seen God's provision as miraculously and hilariously paraded before me as it was that day. The experience created a kind of crisis in me, as firsthand encounters with the miraculous always do. We cannot walk away from them unchanged. A miracle unveils God's presence and invites us to know Him personally in a new way. This miracle was a direct invitation in my life, an invitation to *know* that God loved me. I had heard that He loved me thousands of times, and I had said it myself hundreds more. But God wanted me to know that He loved me so deeply that His signs would ultimately reorder all of my expectations about God's good dealings, even to the point of my own sense of value.

Unraveling of Lies

For me, the process of reordering my expectations with the revelation of God's love exposed a deep-seated, low self-worth that had shaped me from childhood. Throughout that process, God continued to use money as a handle to bring me in touch with the deep longings, hurts and fears of my soul. I began to see that my money-handling skills, or neglect of them, were reflected in my own self-talk. I was worthless to myself, and I re-created that reality around me. I was careless with my resources just as I was careless with my own self-identity.

The recognition of my low self-worth began to expose other lies and bondages in my life. God drew my attention to other areas of destructive behavior—behavior that pointed to the existence of wounds in my heart. The revelation of the wounds was itself profound; even more so was the revelation that these wounds were the source of my bad conduct. This understanding retrained my awareness of how life "flows." Proverbs 4:23 tells us, "Watch over your heart with all diligence, for from it flow the springs of life." Similarly, Proverbs 23:7 says, "For as [a man] thinks within himself, so he is."

For most of my life I had been oriented to control my life by controlling my behavior. But permanent change came only when, in fasting and prayer, I followed the breadcrumb trail of brokenness all the way back to the headwaters of my heart and allowed the Lord to bring restoration and renewal to me there.

As my heart and mind grew healthier, dreams and desires awakened within me. My expectations began to expand with the truth God was revealing. My encounters with the realm of miracles and healing shouted the reality that *nothing is impossible*. I was becoming a prosperous soul. When I recognized this, I knew I had finally found what had been missing in all my years of teaching and counseling. The substance and message of the prosperous soul emerged in my writing, in conversations, in teaching and then it overtook my life completely. It was as though I had finally awakened from an unknown slumber and found myself taking a new, higher road to what the Bible calls *life more abundant*.

Teaching Transformation

In this process of being overtaken by the prosperity of soul, I put my head together with a friend to dream up a financial class built on the core value of *transformative power*. This core value required class members to do more than parrot sound biblical advice. Paul exhorted us to be "transformed by the renewing of your mind" (Romans 12:2). The implication is twofold: First, new information and ideas, though vital, aren't enough in themselves to transform us. Our very faculty of thought must be made new. Second, we live life from the inside out. Our behavior will permanently change only when our minds change. We understood *renewal* to be the work of the Holy Spirit. Thus, the goal of the class was not merely to provide people with great information, but also to lead them into encounters with the Holy Spirit in which they could experience His renewal in their minds and hearts.

The class essentially invited people into the same process I had undergone—recognizing that money serves as a tool to reveal the issues of one's soul, and that these issues are a garden in which God loves to work. I named the class *Prosperous Soul*. The "prosperous soul" derives from another verse that speaks of our inner life setting the pace for our outer lives, captured by the prayer of the apostle John:

> Beloved, I pray that in all respects you may prosper and be in good health, just as your soul prospers.
>
> 3 John 2

This is a prayer of alignment, of agreement, of likeness. John prayed that our material success and physical health would express the same quality as that of our souls: *prosperity*. If we are to prosper and be in good health *just as* our souls prosper, then the first question naturally is: What is a prosperous soul? I am aware that for some Christians the term "prosperous soul," like many other biblically derived terms, has become so common and familiar that its depth of meaning is obscured. But like all truths, the "prosperous soul" can never be exhausted. One goal of this book is to reopen this deep well of meaning.

The quest to answer the question, "What is a prosperous soul?" initially led me down fruitless paths. My natural orientation for formulas, principles and algorithms compelled me to discover a concise definition for the term that would circumscribe its nature and scope. My approach was scientific. I thought that by reducing the concept of a prosperous soul to a definition, I would be able to study the subject as a dispassionate observer. I mistakenly thought I ought to remain as impartial and unbiased as possible. It wasn't long until I discovered how impossible it is to draw natural lines around an eternal concept like a *prosperous soul*. As I wrestled with this problem, I realized that the Holy Spirit wasn't expecting me to discover a hard-and-fast definition, but an illustrative description. Descriptions can illustrate something indefinable, whereas definitions cannot. Jesus affirms this in the way He taught about the Kingdom of God, using parables and stories of natural things to illustrate something as indefinable as eternity.

Yet Jesus always combined His descriptions of the Kingdom with firsthand experience with the Kingdom, especially through miracles. He revealed that eternal concepts are more than concepts—they are realities. And not only is it impossible to contain such realities within definitions; it is impossible to know them without personal experience. Christ's ministry was a divine *show and tell*, and I believe it is the model for how His followers are to teach the Kingdom.

The need for both preaching and demonstration becomes apparent when we consider the goal of Jesus' teaching. He did not describe the Kingdom and give people tastes of its power in order to draw a crowd, or merely to help those He healed to overcome their difficulties. His ministry culminated in His death and resurrection, which made a complete life transformation available to all who believe. In this new life, He declared, "The kingdom of God is *within you*" (Luke 17:21, NIV, emphasis mine). *Telling and showing* lead to *becoming the living manifestation* of the Kingdom as its reality is born within us.

Jesus reserved His strongest rebukes for those who were stuck on the idea that possessing information and knowledge *about* God was what God desired. Embracing this belief actually leads us to resist the transforming work of God within us, as the Pharisees exemplify. Sadly, we live in a culture in which stuffing ourselves with information is the hallmark of learning. Precious little attention is given to *how* we think and behave, which are the fruits of our spiritual lives. Often it takes some crisis to confront us with the reality that all our knowledge has not led us into encounters with God where we receive His grace to grow in His character.

This book is designed to provoke your heart and spirit to undertake a journey, a voyage. In addition to sharing the insights and experiences that have shaped me, I will share stories and testimonies that illustrate the nature and reality of the prosperous soul and address the spirits of Poverty and Mammon and ways to develop supernatural stewardship. I will also provide you with some biblically inspired prayers and declarations for entering into encounters with the Holy Spirit.

Sozo and Other Tools

Several chapters of this book address specific ways Poverty and Mammon infiltrate our thinking and behavior and create destructive patterns of bondage in our lives. Since these spirits influence all of us, I have no doubt you will recognize their effects in your own life as you read about them—in fact, that is precisely my purpose. With that goal in mind, I will present you with some of the tools that have brought significant breakthrough and healing in my own life and the lives of many others.

At Bethel there is an inner healing and deliverance ministry called *Sozo*. *Sozo* is a Greek word that means "to save," but a brief word study reveals the many dimensions of its meaning throughout the New Testament. This "saving" includes physical and emotional healing, deliverance from demonic torment and forgiveness of sin. *Sozo* implies that the salvation Christ purchased for us creates access to the total restoration of our bodies, minds and spirits. It does this by restoring us to our relationship with Father God, which also in turn restores us to our true identity and purpose. As Bethel Sozo ministry's website describes it:

> The Sozo ministry is a unique inner healing and deliverance ministry in which the main aim is to get to the root of those things hindering your personal connection with the Father, Son and Holy Spirit. With a healed connection with the Father, Son and Holy Spirit, you can walk in the destiny to which you have been called.[1]

The typical Sozo session involves a time of prayer in which those trained in this ministry facilitate an interaction between a person and God. Unlike traditional counseling, the person receiving the ministry does not have to talk about every detail of his or her situation. The ministers have some basic tools, developed from accumulated experience and revelation, of how lies and bondages typically develop in people's lives. And their task is to allow the Holy Spirit to guide them and the person receiving ministry in applying those tools for the emotional, physical and spiritual healing of that individual. Sozo is a very personal and powerful experience in which the Holy Spirit is ever faithful to show up and bring revelation, healing and a deeper connection to the one receiving ministry.[2]

While I am not able to create an identical scenario in a book as in a class, I have adapted some Sozo tools for you in this book. These are essentially scripted prayers and declarations designed to help you interact with the Lord on your issues. Scripture provides plenty of evidence that confessing agreement with truth, both vocally and with actions, is a powerful catalyst for establishing that truth in our lives. I strongly encourage you to use these tools. I have received many testimonies from class participants who have used them and been led into interactions with the Holy Spirit that brought revelation and breakthrough.

All of these tools are designed to work on your soul, like the ship in the story of the voyage. You will encounter useful financial suggestions and directions throughout the book, yet in my experience, when people come to me for financial advice, the most significant counsel always traces back to issues of the soul—issues such as self-worth, hope and expectation for good or evil. Unless I address the realm of the soul, I am convinced my words and teaching will have little lasting benefit, for Jesus made it clear it is our souls that are at stake in this life: "For what does it profit a man to gain the whole world, and forfeit his soul?" (Mark 8:36).

Success

As I described, undertaking the voyage of supernatural stewardship will require your capacity, your ship, to grow and expand throughout the journey. I want to start exploring this picture of growth by considering the word *prosper*. *Prosper* means "to succeed in material terms," or simply "to make successful." When applied to the realm of the soul, the term *success* can seem a bit awkward. How is a prosperous soul successful? And what is success in terms of our souls?

I have written and rewritten my own description of success over the years. Its meaning changed as I worked to complete a college degree, struggled to get ahead in life and watched my children become adults and meet their own challenges. Through this process, I have seen that success cannot be defined by a single achievement or goal because those are fluid and evolving as we progress through life. I have also come to understand that God doesn't define success as a series of achievements. Though it may seem, when you first come to know God, that He is primarily interested in what you are *doing*, there is something He is actually more interested in. Success, in God's terms, is defined entirely by *becoming* a certain kind of person—in fact, by becoming like Christ.

It is a mystery of faith that we don't become like Christ by doing; rather, we enter by faith into the reality that we are already in Him and already like Him. Increasingly our behavior comes to reflect this reality. Peter declared that we "have been born again not of seed which is perishable but imperishable" (1 Peter 1:23). God has put His own eternal DNA in us, and it is replicating a pattern within us: the likeness of His Son. No matter how imperceptible that likeness may be at any point in our lives, it is growing, expanding and developing continually.

God gives us some powerful keys as to how this likeness develops. One is the renewing of the mind, as we've seen, which works in tandem with the truth that *as we think in our hearts, so are we*. Another related key is that *we become what we behold*. Paul declares, "But we all, with unveiled face, beholding as in a mirror the glory of the Lord, are being transformed into the same image from glory to glory, just as from the Lord, the Spirit" (2 Corinthians 3:18).

Something powerful happens when you fix your gaze on the One in whose image you were made. You change from glory to glory. And at some point in that process, the scales tip. You become aware of a "critical mass" of the life of Christ in you. You realize that His life is working out a divine purpose within you that is greater and more powerful than any weakness, lie, scheme or obstacle. You actually *know* that "greater is He who is in you than he who is in the world" (1 John 4:4).

Your purpose is in you as grain is in wood. Though damaged or hidden, the grain remains; the two are one. You can deny your purpose, mistake it or even forsake it, yet it remains. And if you work with it and build upon it—if you align your gaze and your thinking with the truth of who you are in Christ—it's like plugging yourself into an electric socket. You discover an inexhaustible reservoir of energy and courage. Struggles may arise, but they are defeated. Distractions, temptations and plots against you become irrelevant. You become like Nehemiah, who said to his enemies, "I am doing a great work and I cannot come down. Why should the work stop while I leave it and come down to you?" (Nehemiah 6:3). Purpose creates not arrogance but vitality, focus, courage.

It is my hope that you will get in touch with the power of purpose in the pages of this book, particularly as we explore the influences of Poverty and Mammon. I have learned that the most powerful strategy for overcoming these influences is to fix your gaze upon the reality of your destiny to become like Christ, and not upon lies and dangers, which so quickly become magnified when you give them attention. One of the most powerful skills you can learn as a Christian is to practice a kind of holy denial toward everything that distracts you from fixing your gaze upon Jesus. If you simply give your full attention to the reality of the life of the Son of God within you, growing into a mature expression of your purpose, it gradually becomes impossible to live with small vision, low expectations, fear or negative self-worth. Likewise, the appeal of a lifestyle governed by an ascetic, brute-force regimen for controlling your financial life (or any other area of behavior) will fade away entirely. This is what Paul refers to in Colossians:

These are matters which have, to be sure, the appearance of wisdom in self-made religion and self-abasement and severe treatment of the body, *but are* of no value against fleshly indulgence.

Colossians 2:23, emphasis mine

Those artificial limits shrink and diminish you, whereas the life of Christ in you, by its very nature, is exactly what He said: *abundant* (see John 10:10). To contain it, you must *expand*.

Bethel Pastor Bill Johnson regularly points out, "The Christian life was always meant to be known for its passions more than its disciplines." He explains that disciplines are like guardrails on the highway of life that help to keep us on the road. But guardrails cannot provide the fuel that our hearts were made to burn. The problem I see in the lives of many Christians is not that they have failed to establish good financial disciplines, but that the fire in their hearts is not burning hot enough to take them anywhere important. Conversely, I immediately recognize those whose souls are prospering by their passion—not passion expressed in great discipline, but passion expressed in their singleness of purpose. *Success* is seen in the soul that has come alive with divine purpose.

Stewardship

Purpose is the ingredient perhaps most lacking from much teaching on Christian stewardship. Without a clear vision of the purposes for which God has entrusted us to steward our lives and possessions, we inevitably adopt a slavish, task-oriented approach to life. We tithe, save, give offerings and provide for our families because God told us to. Certainly, we may experience the rewards for such obedience on some level—no one denies that it feels good to give to worthy causes, to take care of those we love and to achieve financial goals. But people who don't know God practice such things and experience the same results. If that is all there is to it, we would do just as well getting our financial advice from Suze Orman or Dr. Phil.

As I indicated in my parable, the One who has commissioned us on this voyage of life has a purpose and desire that is far more important, more interesting and more *relational* than an account of stewardship focusing merely on disciplines. God wants partners. I didn't originate this idea with my parable—Jesus did it with His. He used a parable of stewardship to describe the way His Kingdom comes: By giving His servants money to handle, the Master is looking to find those who can rule faithfully with Him in His Kingdom (see Luke 19:11–27). The reward of faithfulness is to share in the King's authority—in fact, to be part of His family business. Our stewardship is "training for reigning."

As we see in most areas of life, we train for something simply by doing it. We can learn a lot *about* something without doing it, but we only learn to do it by doing it. A tennis player trains by playing tennis, a singer trains by singing, and a leader trains by leading. If we are training to reign with Christ, then we train by learning to reign with Him now—and reigning, or *dominion*, is to be the hallmark of our stewardship.

This shouldn't surprise us. Scripture is clear that we are to *reign in life*: "For if by the transgression of the one, death reigned through the one, much more those who receive the *abundance* of grace and of the gift of righteousness will *reign in life* through the One, Jesus Christ" (Romans 5:17, emphasis mine). Notice the connection between *abundance* and *reigning*. This linkage is obvious in all levels of life. With the limitation of resources comes the limitation of effect.

Conversely, a powerful person is one who has access to great resources. Our purpose to walk in dominion cannot be separated from our purpose to walk in abundance.

The resources that we need to reign in life, according to Paul, are spiritual, not material—"grace and . . . the gift of righteousness." These are the "true riches" of which Jesus spoke. And yet there is a clear relationship between our use of material resources and spiritual resources. Jesus asked, "Therefore if you have not been faithful in the unrighteous mammon, who will commit to your trust the true riches?" (Luke 16:11, NKJV).

Money—"unrighteous mammon"—is a gauge for all of us. As we see in Jesus' parable and in this verse, God uses our faithfulness with money as an index of our spiritual faithfulness in general. We also see that faithfulness is the key to true abundance. Where we may get confused is in interpreting what Jesus wants us to do about money. We may think that if we detect unfaithfulness in our spending, we need to work on being more faithful with money. But Jesus' question indicates that our use of finances points to something deeper. Faithfulness is defined by our purpose and the One who gave it to us. If unfaithfulness is found in our use of funds, this indicates an underlying, more fundamental unfaithfulness to God and to our purpose. We must work, therefore, on the level of our purpose and our relationship with God if we are to put our money, and our lives, in order. That is the voyage to becoming a prosperous soul.

2

Trouble with Money

The message of our call to be prosperous souls and supernatural stewards has been growing in me for years. But the impetus to write this book came upon me strongly in the end as it became clearer than ever that we live in a society permeated with the mishandling of money. We've all read the headlines: Foreclosures and bankruptcies. Unemployment and company failures. Stimulus packages and dire market fluctuations. As we look at the national and global economies, it seems the repercussions of the times are likely to reverberate for years to come—years that will likely look very different from the past two decades, which have reflected an apparent increasing affluence.

In times of financial uncertainty, people have to make significant choices about what they believe and how they behave. At present, many thousands are coping with the loss of retirement savings, homes, jobs and hopes. For them, Plan A has failed, and the task of fabricating Plan B is daunting for many reasons. For one, if they are going to come up with a plan that is better, they will need to find out why Plan A failed. For another, they will need to find their options for doing things differently next time around. Both tasks take time, energy and courage to face the truth. Some people will rise to the occasion, finding a way through their difficult but necessary challenges. But others, even in the midst of their losses, will just keep their heads down and try to get on with business as usual.

For Christians, business as usual is not an option. I contend that seasons of instability like the present one are always important opportunities to awaken us. They test our priorities and call us to freshly engage with our biblical purpose to be salt and light in the world. If we consider just a few key features of the recent financial crisis, we'll see clearly our responsibility to seek wisdom for being a good steward in the culture around us.

One reality made obvious by the recent financial crisis is that a good number of the "experts" leading our federal and financial institutions have not been acting so expertly. The credit and housing bubbles that mushroomed in the early 2000s were inflated as banks increased lending and government removed or failed to enforce regulations on lending. This allowed for the dangerous tendencies in our debt-based culture to be expressed. While those tendencies had been developing for a while, like a frog slowly cooking in a pot, the authorities seriously failed to control the bubble in the past decade. Ask someone who was around in the 1960s about debt and they'll give you a sense of how much our policies and borrowing habits have changed. Abandoning historic limits, the government has led the way in embracing big spending and big debt. Americans used to avoid debt whenever possible and save their money. In the 2000s we accelerated the tendency of the past few decades to quit saving and increasingly tolerate debt. We took it on in unprecedented proportions in order to experiment with the idea promoted by "experts" that leveraging is an inspired tool for creating wealth.

For a while, the experiment seemed to be working. All that credit did seem to be making a way for many Americans to "get ahead" financially. The middle class discovered apparent gold mines of equity in their homes, and they took the chance to grab at their dreams: larger houses, newer cars, longer vacations and bigger college loans. In the unusually sustained growth of the housing and credit bubbles, the commonsense concern that "what goes up must come down" simply diminished. Indeed, it lulled many into thinking the sky was the limit. Some assumed their homes were as good as savings accounts and cashed out their reserves accordingly. Meanwhile, the Wall Street casino had been building its colossal house of cards in new financial products, such as mortgage-backed securities, derivatives and credit default swaps, a house entirely built on the backs of debtors. Investors the world over risked billions on the assumption that we would pay our ballooning mortgages, hoping to get as rich as possible before the market turned. Though the warning signs of collapse were there for anyone to find, it seems most were having too much fun to care. The temporary benefits created by risk-laden means clouded the view of the disastrous ends that would come.

Here's the "official" version given by the Group of Twenty in the Declaration of the Summit on Financial Markets and the World Economy:

> During a period of strong global growth, growing capital flows, and prolonged stability earlier this decade, market participants sought higher yields without an adequate appreciation of the risks and failed to exercise proper due diligence. At the same time, weak underwriting standards, unsound risk

management practices, increasingly complex and opaque financial products, and consequent excessive leverage combined to create vulnerabilities in the system. Policy-makers, regulators and supervisors, in some advanced countries, did not adequately appreciate and address the risks building up in financial markets, keep pace with financial innovation, or take into account the systemic ramifications of domestic regulatory actions.[1]

Some analysts have described this crisis as the "perfect storm." But, as is clear in this statement, the storm was entirely man-made. Some involved acted with good intentions, while others were found to have acted badly, even criminally. Some were ignorant about risk, while others had a fair idea of what they were taking on. My purpose is not to identify and analyze all the choices involved. I simply want to exploit this mess to remind Christians of a basic truth: Without divine wisdom and courage, human beings, no matter how well-intentioned and educated, are bound to fail. Our plans may seem to work for a while, creating "growth" and "stability." But lasting growth and stability can only be built on one foundation, and it's not the one we've been using.

As Christian financial teachers have pointed out for years, a debt-based economy is fundamentally flawed because it produces bondage. Debt is bondage. Proverbs 22:7 states, "The borrower becomes the lender's slave." The dark truth behind our status as a wealthy nation is that on paper we own almost nothing. Even those who are debt free live under the shadow of a national debt that breaks down to hundreds of thousands of dollars per person, numbers that only keep growing. We may live very comfortably, but at the end of the day we all *work for the bank*. Our "private property" is on loan. And despite appearances, the bank is making out pretty well these days. It has been in the interest of big business and banks to keep us indentured to the cycle of endless consumption subsidized by debt. But rarely have consumers been so uncritically willing to sign up for it. The bottom line is we want stuff. We want the latest stuff. And we want it now.

Debt and conspicuous consumption are the core of our economic foundation, and both are problematic. We may console ourselves with the idea that free markets have increased wealth across the world, and it is certainly true that more and more people have increasing access to consumer goods. However, our consumer culture sabotages many of the ways this increase might benefit the many more who are still in need. For instance, we are awash in marketing propaganda that tells us we ought to spend our money on our appetites for food, sex, status, entertainment and power. (Notice the term *good* has been redefined in our economy to mean a commodity, something that makes a profit. Pornography, drugs, weapons and other destructive products are thus added to the list of "goods" fulfilling supply and demand and performing what we perceive to be the all-important task: stimulating the economy.) As a result, our mounting debts constrain our ability to give, both as individuals and as a nation. In reality, the Western version of wealth-evangelism has only offered the world a place at the table of debt and consumption. Negative economic cycles are normal, but when combined with the vast foreign holdings of U.S. Treasury securities (debt), these cycles are exaggerated, creating uncertainties for both our own welfare and that of our foreign investing neighbors. The economies of many Third World countries are currently languishing under their obligations to Western banks and U.S. Treasury obligations.

While lending and consuming are part of any economy, and are not inherently wrong in themselves, we have taken them far beyond the bounds of health and sustainability. And we have emphasized them above other important economic practices such as producing, saving and giving. This perversion is an expression of moral flaws that have been allowed to take hold in our culture, flaws that run deeper and create greater risks than the ones we observe on Wall Street. Until these deeper issues are addressed, there is little hope of anyone coming up with a different Plan B. Granted, people have admitted that the notion of "moral hazard" has characterized the recent financial crisis and that more limits and regulations might have prevented its magnitude. But contrary to popular opinion, "moral hazard" is not created so much by flaws in our social structures as by the choices of individuals. And because our social institutions do not have the power to make us moral people, the only kinds of restraint they can offer us are the kinds that destroy genuine freedom. People who are in bondage to their own greed, lust and pride can only be regulated by external forms of bondage.

The Church is the only entity equipped to penetrate to the spiritual roots of our moral illnesses. We are to call out the fruit of the Holy Spirit in the economy, enlisting the weapons of love, joy, patience, goodness, kindness and self-control, which are the foundation of true freedom. Many Christian teachers rightly point out that our society's willingness to take on the slavery of debt in exchange for stuff is an expression of the deep emptiness that people are seeking to fill within themselves. One of the most powerful aspects of the Gospel is that this emptiness can only be filled by the loving reconnection with the Father that Jesus offers. For this reason, it is less critical that we condemn the world's decadence than that we make an appeal to human *desire* and how it is genuinely fulfilled. Jesus had plenty to say about sin, hell and judgment, but the main thing He came to say was, "Good news!" He offers true freedom, true health and true riches to any and all who would come to Him. One of the prophetic names for Christ is the *Desired of all Nations* (see Haggai 2:7, NIV). If the nations do not desire Christ, it is because they have not yet encountered Him as He truly is; they continue to mistake other things for the true object of their desires. This makes it our responsibility as His Body on earth to become an authentic representation of Him, so the world finally discovers that for which it truly hungers.

Perhaps as you have examined your own financial circumstances, or considered the economic injustices and evils in the world, you have cried out, as I did, with Gideon: "Why then has all this happened to us? And where are all [God's] miracles which our fathers told us about?" (Judges 6:13). God's answer to us, as it has been in every generation, is the same as the word He gave to Gideon. He calls us to partner with Him to become the answer to our own questions. His strategy is to reveal Himself as the Desired of all Nations by calling out "a holy nation" (1 Peter 2:9), a people who learn to seek and experience Him as the true fulfillment of their desires. Answering this call is not something we do all at once. It is a process, one of detaching our desires from the false things to which we've attached them and redirecting them toward truly worthwhile things, which are all found in Christ.

Fall of Babylon

Learning to relate to money in a new way is a significant part of the process of retraining our desires. If God uses money as a tool to cultivate our heart and develop in us a prosperous soul, it is because money is a tool on which we often place our trust. Our application of finance is a clear indication of who or what we trust to meet our needs and desires. In fact, the word *credit* comes from the Latin word meaning "belief,

43

trust." When a lender extends credit to a borrower, it creates a bond of trust between them, an obligation and a promise. Every transaction between a buyer and seller is an act of trust, not only in one another, but also in those who issue our credit and our currency. As acts of faith, our financial agreements have deep spiritual, moral and social implications.

However, this interconnectedness we create by credit is more complicated than simply loaning your neighbor a hammer and expecting him to return it. In modern banking, the saver expects two important benefits: interest and security. Interest means that his or her savings deposit is growing (hopefully faster than the rate of inflation). Security means that with the passage of time, the savings plus interest will be there when he or she wants it back. For the bank, however, this deposit relationship is very different. Banks take this deposit and lend it to your neighbor, charge a higher interest rate for the use of the loan, keep most of the interest for themselves, and finally pay you what little is left over. Further, the bank is allowed to grant more credit than they actually hold in cash. This is called a *multiple* and greatly increases the interest for themselves. The multiple is one of the very powerful ways that a bank creates money. And while I said earlier that lending and consuming are part of any economy, and are not inherently wrong in themselves, I will add here what is wrong: the intentional and systematic enslavement of consumers. By creating artificial demand through marketing and propaganda, people are drawn into debt beyond their capacity to pay. Money is no longer working for them; they are working for money—and I call this bondage. Living beyond our means, family by family, causes a national, and eventually international, debt crisis to emerge.

I do not need to vilify bankers; responsibility ultimately rests with us as consumers. We must remember it is the consumers who agree to follow unwise offers of indebtedness. Similar to the Egyptians in Joseph's day, we sell ourselves into bondage in exchange for our "goodies." Though we believe we are celebrating our individual freedoms, we are actually practicing something else, evidenced by our willingness to choose excessive debt.

Once again, I submit that our abuse of money is creating nothing less than slavery, as Proverbs described—the borrowers are slaves of the lenders. We are in bondage, bondage that is primarily spiritual and moral. Scripture concludes such bondage is a demonic influence. If we look closely, the current global economy is manifesting the influence of what the Bible calls *Babylon*, a satanic power system characterized by sensuality, greed and slavery:

> I saw another angel coming down from heaven . . . and he cried out with a mighty voice, saying, "Fallen, fallen is Babylon the great! . . . For all the nations have drunk of the wine of the passion of her immorality, and the kings of the earth have committed acts of immorality with her, and the merchants of the earth have become rich by the wealth of her sensuality." I heard another voice from heaven, saying, "Come out of her, my people, so that you will not participate in her sins and receive of her plagues; for her sins have piled up as high as heaven, and God has remembered her iniquities." . . . And the merchants of the earth weep and mourn over her, because no one buys their cargoes any more—cargoes of gold and silver and precious stones and pearls and fine linen and purple and silk and scarlet, and every kind of citron wood and every article of ivory and every article made from very costly wood and bronze and iron and marble, and cinnamon and spice and incense and perfume and frankincense and wine and olive oil and fine flour and wheat and cattle and sheep, and cargoes of horses and chariots and slaves and human lives.
>
> Revelation 18:1–5, 11–13

This passage indicates that the influence of Babylon operates primarily through political and financial agreements. The governments and merchants of the world's nations bind their citizens in immorality as they exchange their cargoes, which include, most notably, "slaves and human lives." I find it significant that the earliest forms of banking first grew up over 3,000 years ago in Mesopotamia, the site of ancient Babylon.[2]

As the Church offers people a way out of bondage under this spirit, we must be completely free of its influence ourselves. But what exactly does that mean? Do we participate in the system of agreements with Babylon every time we use a credit card, and if so, are we coming under bondage? I do think it's possible to participate in our financial systems without letting our hearts become enslaved to "stuff," but once again, maintaining this freedom grows more difficult the more we embrace a lifestyle of debt. Christian financial teachers who emphasize getting out of and avoiding debt are not only being biblically correct and sensible, they are showing us a practical way to resist the Babylonian spirit. If you have endeavored to get out of debt and live debt free in our culture, my guess is that it has required you to grapple with your desires for instant gratification, for the latest and greatest and for stuff in general. These are some of the desires Babylon manipulates in order to lead us into bondage.

But what about the use of money in general? Is money good or evil? Money is actually one of the most brilliant human inventions. By simply making a collective agreement to assign value to a certain substance or object (historically this has included everything from gold and silver to shells, beads and sticks), a society is able to grease the flow of trade and thus create stability and vitality. That is the purpose of money. In essence, money is a very powerful idea that binds people together and accommodates their lives. But when money is perverted from its original purpose, it causes problems. The same tool that has the power to help has the power to harm, depending on who is wielding it and for what purpose.

Because money is a form of power, it creates a way for the desires and motives of our hearts to be expressed. We are in a season in which the prosperity of our nation is revealing the waywardness of our hearts. The best and brightest of our national and global leaders are directing us further down the path of greed, oppression and injustice. Many are well-intentioned but fail to account for the moral and spiritual compromises that inevitably undercut their most sophisticated strategies. Just as the integrity of a building is compromised when it fails to withstand a certain level of pressure, we live in a world that is compromised because it has failed to handle the pressure of increasing wealth.

If we are to provide solutions to the world's troubles with money, the Church must succeed where the world has failed in handling wealth. In addition to training our desires to seek our true object, Christ, we must resist the false happiness and bondage of Babylon. In other words, Babylon must fall in our individual hearts before it will fall in reality. We must test our own hearts by learning to master money and use it according to its true purpose. Merely ignoring the role of money and material resources won't cause the wayward motives of our hearts to go away; we'll just have fewer opportunities for those bad motives to be expressed. Instead, we must realize that mastering wealth is a key element of testing and proving our character. For some of us, the test of wealth may be to give it all away, as Christ instructed the rich young ruler. For most of us, I believe, Christ would have us learn to master wealth in many different ways—in saving, in giving and in investing. Moreover, I believe some of us are called, as Joseph was, to carry out a supernatural strategy for stewarding the wealth of nations—for "the saving of many lives" (Genesis 50:20, NIV).

Mastering Ourselves

Joseph suffered thirteen years of hardship, loss, persecution and abandonment. But God understood the pressures that Joseph's character needed to withstand in order to succeed once he was promoted to rule over Egypt. God had marked Joseph to preside over the most powerful nation of his time, administrating a massive transfer of wealth for the purpose of ensuring the survival and future of Israel. But before that, he learned to walk in authority and stewardship, first in Potiphar's house and later in prison. Joseph undoubtedly learned much about stewardship under Potiphar, who himself was a steward over Pharaoh's household. Then in prison Joseph was appointed by the head jailer to manage the whole prison. Joseph's soul and character had to be purified and strengthened through these tests in managing what was another's. Otherwise, he would not have had the capacity and wisdom to stand in a place of authority and power to manage the wealth of a vast nation such as Egypt.

However, there is a vital element in Joseph's success that we cannot overlook; in fact, I have devoted a later chapter entirely to this element. That element is the *dream*. The dreams of Joseph were visions of his destiny, the magnification of his purpose. As a young man, Joseph saw himself standing in a position of authority. This was the purpose he carried in his heart through all his years of struggle, to the end of his life. If Joseph hadn't understood his purpose to walk in authority, he would have missed the opportunities presented by his circumstances to grow in that purpose.

God can use any circumstance in our lives to shape and develop the divine purpose He has placed within us. And our divine purpose has much in common with Joseph's, for God calls all believers to stand in a sphere and measure of authority and power in life. It is precisely this authority and power that position us to bring the "true riches"—the abundance and solutions of the Kingdom of God—to the world around us, as Joseph did. The important question for us is whether we will embrace that purpose, which in its nature is a call to greatness, to excellence, to pioneering. It is a call to increase our capacity to carry more, that we might have something to give to others.

Unfortunately, many believers see themselves as victims of circumstance, surrounded by lack and a bondage to debt that no amount of hard work can eliminate. They may know that isn't the best God has for them, but they aren't exactly sure what God does have for them. They understand the basics—that they are supposed to work hard, provide for their families and tithe, and can expect this to position them for God's blessing in some way. After all, isn't that how the promises of God work? He tells us how to cooperate with His way of doing things and promises that we can expect His blessings as a result.

That is indeed what God means by His promises. But what does it mean to cooperate with God's ways? It means living in the revelation of divine purpose. Without a revelation of divine purpose, we don't understand *why* we ought to take care of our families, *why* we ought to work hard, *why* God wants to bless us. Without a revelation of divine purpose, obedience becomes just another survival technique. We obey God so we can spiritually survive, just as we go to work to obtain a wage to buy the groceries, pay the bills and survive.

God's divine purpose for each of us is not ultimately to obey a set of instructions. Rather, His purpose is that we *become* like Him, for imitation is the highest form of worship. Moreover, He tells us that in Christ, we *are already* like Him, and thus our primary assignment is to pursue a relationship of abiding in Him, through which we will increasingly express that likeness (see 1 John 2:24). When we live with this purpose, it shapes our approach to any instruction He has given us for life. We tithe, for example, not simply because He told us to. Neither do we tithe because we trust that it benefits us to obey God. We tithe because in doing so we are being like God and we are partnering with God to support His work on earth.

Living in the revelation of our divine purpose also shapes our vision of God's blessings in our lives. Most of us expect blessings to be *stuff*. But God wants us to expect far more than that. God wants us to ask and expect Him to give us Himself. He wants us to discover and live in the divine wisdom by which He created us. We were not designed for survival. We were designed for Him. When we have Him, we have everything.

Of course, being designed for God goes both ways: We do not have Him unless He has us. The way of the prosperous soul is learning to step into this dance; it means fully yielding all to God, and fully receiving all that He is and has as He shares Himself with us. It is the way of love. The more we come to know the Father's love for us, the more we embrace a level of relationship where God is so much more than merely the provider for our needs and wants. God's deepest desire is for mature sons and daughters who will love Him and join Him in what He is doing.

I said earlier that learning to handle wealth is a key to developing our character. It is even more accurate to say that maturing in integrity and character is a matter of learning to live in abundance. A classic New Testament example is Paul's testimony:

> I know how to get along with humble means, and I also know how to live in prosperity; in any and every circumstance I have learned the secret of being filled and going hungry, both of having abundance and suffering need. I can do all things through Him who strengthens me.
>
> Philippians 4:12–13

External circumstances were never the determining factor in Paul's choices. He always made choices according to the boundless resources of Christ's strength in him, and his ability to access this strength in any situation was the mark of his maturity.

Another example is found in the Sermon on the Mount. Jesus commanded us to be "perfect," which means mature and complete, lacking in nothing. He then described what perfection looks like:

> "I say to you, love your enemies and pray for those who persecute you, so that you may be sons of your Father who is in heaven; for He causes His sun to rise on the evil and the good, and sends rain on the righteous and the unrighteous. For if you love those who love you, what reward do you have? Do not even the tax collectors do the same? If you greet only your brothers, what more are you doing than others? Do not even the Gentiles do the same? Therefore you are to be perfect, as your heavenly Father is perfect."
>
> Matthew 5:44–48

The mature son or daughter is one who has learned to access and release the abundance of the Father's love, without condition, to every person he or she meets. This is the consummate definition of integrity. This is what it means to be like God. This is how we reveal the reality of the Kingdom of God, which is always increasing (see Isaiah 9:7), in the midst of a world that is always cycling through advance and decline.

A New Mind

Some years ago, my wife and I decided to experiment with our spending. We recognized a pattern in our marriage in which our needs continually *outgrew* our provision. It seemed every time an increase came along, whether through a pay raise or unexpected income, we neatly and efficiently found a way to spend that increase. We dubbed this the *potted-plant syndrome*, because a plant will always expand to the size of its pot until it is "root bound." It will then struggle in a capacity crisis until it is repotted, only to begin the desperate cycle again. Our finances made us feel like root-bound plants.

We couldn't understand why we were in this condition. Anyone looking in would see only evidence of success. We had a beautiful home, reliable vehicles and a well-stocked pantry. Yet we both felt we could find better ways to honor God with our money.

We began our experiment as a mutual agreement to stop expanding our lifestyle to fill our pot. We started by trimming expenses and bolstering incomes, and we lived contentedly and simply. We prayed for blessing (see 1 Chronicles 4:10) and began sowing seed generously whenever we felt God's provocation. Soon, we were living within our means, giving generously and saving a tiny amount from each month toward an emergency fund.

A year passed and we were *repotted*. We received a raise in income. Once or twice during that year we also enjoyed small but unexpected gifts. We were being blessed, but as we were now governing our resources according to our purpose, we held to our simple lifestyle choices. Gradually, the pot increased again. And again. Each time this happened, Dawna and I restrained our desires and stuck to living contentedly, simply and generously. The result: freedom and increased capacity. Now our generosity grew because we had capacity to give. Our debts fell because we were living below our means. And since our meager savings program had created a small emergency fund, we had created a bumper of security around us. Our simple experiment turned out to be a strategy to escape our personal capacity crisis and it became a pathway to live and give more freely and powerfully than ever before.

The solution to our trouble with money was not about lack and want; it was about purpose and perspective. Volumes have been written about trimming our plants, but sacrifice apart from purpose is no sacrifice at all. But paradoxically, true sacrifice for the sake of purpose usually ends up feeling like it's not a sacrifice, for it always brings the reward of greater fulfillment in becoming who we are made to be. For Dawna and me, our corporate "Yes" to pursue God initially became "No" to some of our wants. But as we walked in our commitment, we saw and felt God's pleasure and favor as He increased the pot and satisfied our deeper desire to partner with Him in blessing those around us.

People with prosperous souls—people who practice accessing the abundance of the Kingdom in every circumstance—think differently from the way others do. Their reasoning is founded on a completely different reality. One of the most profound statements of such reasoning comes from Paul:

> He who did not spare His own Son, but delivered Him over for us all, how will He not also with Him freely give us all things?
>
> Romans 8:32

If you have God, you have everything. If you've received the Father's gift of Christ, you have no reason to think or act as if you lack anything. We mature in Christ by leaving behind our old worries over what we need and boldly giving our full attention to this gift. It was for this reason that Paul urgently and almost impatiently exhorted the Corinthian church to leave immaturity and wake up to the truth that would lead them to maturity:

> All things belong to you, whether Paul or Apollos or Cephas or the world or life or death or things present or things to come; all things belong to you, and you belong to Christ; and Christ belongs to God.
>
> 1 Corinthians 3:21–23

If we belong to Christ, all things are ours. This reality has the power to silence every anxiety and impulse that would betray us into bondage to debt and consumption. Moreover, this reality enables us to approach material resources from a position of partnership and dominion rather than compliance and survival. Above all, this reality helps us get our attention off material resources altogether and start learning to access the "true riches" of the Kingdom.

I am convinced only the people who know how to access these "true riches" will provide the answers our national and global leaders are seeking. The time is ripe for a generation of Josephs to rise and silence the magicians, our economic gurus, in their fruitless attempts to interpret what is going on, and release supernatural revelation and strategies for "the saving of many lives."

The question for all of us is whether we will allow this reality—"all things are ours"—to become our reality. This is not the reality we were born into. Slavery, lack and survival were the primary features of our natural habitat before we met Christ. The revolution that the world has always hungered for—the only Plan B that will ever work and has ever worked—is the revolution of those who boldly leave the poverty of earth to seek the abundance of heaven. And this revolution begins in the soul.

3

Spirit of Poverty

As [a man] thinks within himself, so he is.

Proverbs 23:7

A close friend of mine has a daughter who received an amazing gift on her sixteenth birthday. As the girl was walking home after checking the mailbox, a bit dejected from finding it empty of birthday cards, she caught a glint of something on the sidewalk. She didn't have her glasses on, so she almost wrote it off as a sparkle of cement in the summer sun. But something prompted her to stop. When she bent down, she saw a large gemstone wedged in a crack in the sidewalk, as though it had been mounted there. She picked it up, admiring its beauty and perfection. Just then she heard the voice of the Lord say, "Happy birthday, Princess! I love you!"

She brought the gemstone home and showed it to her mother, who tested its quality by using it to scratch a drinking glass. But when they took it to be appraised and later set in a ring, the jewelers who examined it were shocked to discover that it was not a diamond. Based on its properties, they confirmed it to be a flawless gem of an unknown origin. A year later, the daughter found another gem in a parking lot, and that same week her brother found two identical gems on separate occasions while rollerblading—all of them "presented" in cracks in the pavement, like a supernatural egg hunt. My friend's daughter wears her precious ring to this day, and her mother concludes, "God knew how to touch her heart in a special way because He loves us so."

Another friend of mine watched in wonder as God restored his stolen business. This man had been quite successful in the agricultural chemical business until a predatory competitor came along and helped itself to his valuable patents. Bravely, my friend fought back and eventually won in court, but it cost him nearly everything. In the end, he closed the business, hoping simply to rebuild his family, as well as their confidence in justice.

"Then it happened about a year later," he recalled to me. "Before the court battles, I had been involved in negotiations overseas. When I lost the business, I never renewed those negotiations, figuring it was all for naught. Then one day I received an email from one of those foreign business associates. He had contacted me to accept an old negotiation!

"I restarted the business, and it developed a lucrative second life after having burned to the ground. Though a competitor tried to kill it, and I tried to abandon it and time tried to obliterate it, God had other plans. He brought it back to my family to serve us well in these later years of our life. God has a way of finding us even when we're hiding."

These stories have similar beginnings but very different endings from the ones I read about recently in a news article. The article announced: "Poor young rancher wins $232 mil. jackpot." The fortunate 23-year-old from Pierre, South

Dakota, won "one of the biggest undivided jackpots in U.S. lottery history." "I will not squander it," said the young man, who plans to buy a bigger spread and repay the kindnesses of other townspeople who have helped his family.

Contrasting his hopeful outlook with what most often happens to lottery winners, the article went on to describe the fates of two others. A woman from New Jersey had won $5.4 million in the mid-1980s, only to squander the prize within a few years. A winner in West Virginia was awarded $315 million in 2002. According to the article, "Five years later, he was blaming the money for causing his granddaughter's fatal drug overdose, his divorce, his inability to trust, and hundreds of lawsuits to be filed against him." "I don't have any friends," the man said. "Every friend that I've had, practically, has wanted to borrow money or something and, of course, once they borrow money from you, you can't be friends anymore."[1]

I had an experience with the Holy Spirit a few years ago that helped set me on a quest to discover the differences between lottery winners and people like my two friends. It happened at His favorite time for appointments with me: "whine o'clock" in the morning. Perhaps He finds me more open when I'm not quite conscious. On that particular morning, the Spirit asked me, "You've been asking for supernatural provision. What do you think that would look like if you were to receive it?"

The question wandered, lost, until my first cup of coffee. Then I remembered the gold coin in the fish's mouth. What an exciting and efficient supernatural display, I thought—I could pay my bills in a moment's time as I angled for trout with my friends! But after several such scenarios passed through my imagination, something dawned on me. I realized that all my versions of "supernatural provision" had this in common: They were all divine interruptions in circumstance, instantaneous rescues from challenging situations. I anticipated God's provision being something that snatched me away from troubles, or made the troubles melt away, as a genie might do. At that point, I opened my heart to hear what God had to say about this. He showed me, "You're still seeing through eyes of poverty. Prosperity may be different than you think."

Both my friends and the lottery winners experienced sudden provision, and yet they ended up in very different places. They are strong testimonies to the fact that the "supernatural" element I and many others are seeking cannot be found in a dramatic change in circumstance.

Leaving Familiar Shores

In the voyage of the prosperous soul, the first form of supernatural provision we receive is the Merchant's commission, which calls us to leave the islands of Poverty. Though the islands have intimidated and trapped us, this calling provides us with the heavenly courage, desire and faith needed to abandon those familiar shores for the sake of becoming His partners. With His help, we find the will to sail past these perilous shores of Poverty and Mammon, which are systems of lies and distortions designed to deceive and destroy us.

The most powerful weapon against a lie is the truth. Therefore, we are best able to recognize the counterfeit by handling the authentic. The apostle Paul exposed this strategy in his description of spiritual warfare:

> The weapons of our warfare are not of the flesh, but divinely powerful for the destruction of fortresses. We are destroying speculations and every lofty thing raised up against the

knowledge of God, and we are taking every thought captive to the obedience of Christ.

2 Corinthians 10:4–5

The very idea of destroying whatever raises itself against the knowledge of God presupposes that we know God. Likewise, taking our thoughts captive to the obedience of Christ presupposes that we are already on the path of obedience.

We will never get far on the journey of the prosperous soul if our focus is merely on avoiding deception. Rather, we must focus upon seeking to know and obey God. As we do, we will find our discernment growing more finely tuned. The psalmist said, "In Your light we see light" (Psalm 36:9). As the light of the knowledge of God grows in our lives, we not only see Him more fully; we see everything else as it truly is, both good and evil. It is the expanding capacity and prosperity of our souls, as well as the wisdom gained in following the *map* provided by the Holy Spirit that exposes and helps us avoid the hazards of Poverty and Mammon. For this reason, as we explore the nature of Poverty in this chapter, and Mammon in another, I will endeavor to hold them up in the light of the "authentic"—the true prosperity in which God designed us to thrive.

Is Poverty a Spirit?

In some church circles it is not uncommon to hear the phrase "Poverty spirit" or "spirit of Poverty." Perhaps you have heard someone describe a person, community or nation as having a "Poverty spirit." Or perhaps you have been in a prayer meeting where a "spirit of Poverty" was "bound" or "rebuked" or "cast down." Such prayers understandably give rise to the idea there is a "demon of Poverty" that inhabits homes and regions and national geographies. If this were the case, then ending poverty would be a simple matter of casting out a demon of Poverty according to Jesus' command in Matthew 10:8. But deliverance alone is not enough to end poverty. While the spirit of Poverty does involve demonic influence, there is more to it.

The "spirit of Poverty" is not exactly a biblical term. A word study in Scripture will not find "poverty" and "spirit" purposely linked. However, studying each word does help us understand how this phrase has come into use and what is meant by it. "Poverty" (Hebrew *reysh* and Greek *ptocheia*) simply means the state of being poor, being in want or in lack. And while "spirit" (Hebrew *ruach* and Greek *pneuma*) can refer to beings such as angels and demons, as well as to human spirits and the Spirit of God, it also denotes a disposition—an inclination of mind and character. The phrase "Poverty spirit" acknowledges that the experience of lack in a person's life has created an inclination, attitude or "bent" toward poverty in the person.

The basic message of Poverty is this: *There is never enough.* When people live long under the influence of this message, it takes on a personal tone: There is never enough for *me*, because *I am not worth it.* The message of lack attacks us at the deepest level of our identity, value and purpose. Consider how this message gives rise to the following expressions of the Poverty spirit:

- A Poverty spirit creates anxiety or fear. When you live from paycheck to paycheck, you constantly dwell under a black cloud of "that big, unexpected expense." Even after you gain enough to live comfortably, you still worry about losing it all.

- A Poverty spirit hoards token things, mistaking clutter and junk for wealth. You save the fast-food restaurant plastic cup collection. The path in your garage gets narrower every year because you hold on to everything you or your parents ever broke.

- A Poverty spirit believes, *Things just happen to me.* You settle when you should fight. You avoid dreaming about the future because it only reminds you of how powerless you feel to change. You take the path of least resistance and try to grab whatever comfort you can. You perceive yourself as a perpetual victim.

- A Poverty spirit reaches for instant gratification. You make impulse purchases, spending hundreds of dollars on worthless trinkets, yet resist a plan to purchase quality items or make good investments.

- A Poverty spirit hounds you. You feel chased by trouble, while it seems money is chased away from you.

- A Poverty spirit makes you feel enslaved. You see yourself as being ruled by your finances. You have the constant sense you are trapped.

- A Poverty spirit hides you. You find yourself overlooked and ignored. You believe you should be seen and not heard, that your opinion is irrelevant.

- A Poverty spirit chokes out generosity. You may want to give but feel you can't afford to.

- Finally, a Poverty spirit fights to keep you in the same condition. And it causes you to keep others in that condition! If someone has a financial breakthrough, the Poverty spirit in you hopes they lose it. You even take pleasure in the failure of lottery winners!

As is clear in these descriptions, the effects of the Poverty spirit manifest in our financial choices. Yet they are only symptoms of the deeper wounds of our souls in the areas of identity and purpose—the core of who we are. Poverty is not an economic problem; it is a soul-and-spirit problem. *Lack* in any area of our lives, whether for basic needs (food, clothing, shelter), or our more complex needs (opportunities, friendship, affection, knowledge), *bends* the soul and spirit. Once a person has been bent by a Poverty spirit, he may eventually overcome areas of lack, but he can still retain that bent in his soul.

Ask yourself how many of the qualities of the Poverty spirit listed above are at work in our consumer culture. I submit that even in the wealthiest nation in the world, where we can feasibly feed, clothe, shelter and meet many other needs for every citizen within our borders, people still act as though there is never enough. And it is causing a lot of problems.

It's Not What You Have

Now ask yourself how many people you know who are miserable. The word "miserable" comes from the Latin *miser*, which means "wretched." In turn, the English word "miser" is a direct adaptation of the Latin, used to define a "wretched" person as someone who is capable of acquiring and keeping abundance but incapable of using it. Observing a miser is probably one of the clearest ways to see what we mean by a Poverty spirit. A miser does not actually lack on the outside but on the inside. "Bent" by the message of lack, his soul is in utter dissonance with abundance. No matter how much he accumulates, it fails to slake his inner destitution.

You probably know miserable people on both sides of riches—those who have more than enough and those who lack. I certainly have found that people can be rich and miserable just as they can be poor and miserable. Similarly, people can be rich and happy just as they can be poor and happy.

What this reveals is that our attitudes, or "bents"—and consequently the choices these imply—are not determined by our circumstances. Consider the churches of Macedonia: "In a great ordeal of affliction their abundance of joy and their deep poverty overflowed in the wealth of their liberality" (2 Corinthians 8:2). Affliction and poverty were the circumstances, but joy was their attitude, and liberality was what they chose to demonstrate.

In short, people live either happily or miserably regardless of their financial condition or any other circumstance, for that matter. If circumstances do not determine whether we are happy or miserable, then what does? Miserable people, in particular, don't talk about their misery as something they *chose*. Rather, their misery seems an inevitable state, the obvious consequence of pain, guilt, injustice and other evils or hardships they've experienced. We live in a world of suffering. But the truth that our attitudes are independent from circumstances holds up even among those who suffer terrible things. We find survivors who overcome suffering and find healing, forgiveness and joy; likewise, we find victims and offenders who never seem to break free of cycles of abuse, bitterness and pain.

Attitude is something we choose. Many recognize this truth, as well as its importance and power. It gives many people hope they can rise above their circumstances and experience something better in life. Coaches, counselors and even the president of the United States preach that while we may not choose our circumstances, we can always choose our attitude. And attitude will make the difference in our ability to respond well to our circumstances. The important question for all of us is, how do we choose our attitude? Overly simplistic exhortations to "Be Positive" or "Have a Good Attitude" suggest that doing so is all there is to it. But if you've actually tried these methods, you've realized they can fall flat.

Choosing a positive attitude always begs the question, "Why should I be positive?" Choosing an attitude isn't something we can do until we have a reason to support the attitude, and our reasoning is usually built on what we believe to be true about our circumstances. If we believe there is never enough, then it doesn't matter how much we try to be positive. Our inner rationale will always conflict with a positive outlook. If we are going to make any serious change in our attitude, we have to deal with what we believe.

A Paradigm Shift

The "bent" of poverty is a pattern in our souls—a pattern of thinking, feeling and acting based on a set of beliefs about the universe. This set of beliefs is a paradigm that defines our expectations for what we experience and what is possible. It defines our reality. It is like a map, laying out the geography of our world and showing us the various routes available to us through life. On a poverty map, the realities of lack, doubt, insecurity and loss show the journey as limited and scary. Unless we undertake the voyage of the prosperous soul and navigate courageously past the islands of Poverty, we will be confined to the small stretch of sea we've sailed for generations.

Because a poverty paradigm is rooted in a person's core beliefs about himself and the world, it has a very powerful hold. The verse, "As [a man] thinks within himself, so he is" (Proverbs 23:7), speaks to this power. The paradigm that guides our thinking is actually creating and perpetuating our reality. Simply put, our habits of mind define our habits of life. And because we are creatures of habit, one of the most difficult things for us to do is question the reality in which these habits work. The sheer force of doing the same things the same way year after year seems to keep them fixed forever as our personal beliefs. Even the phrase "force of habit" acknowledges that as these ruts in our thinking and behavior develop, we no longer experience them as our choices. They seem to happen on their own. Because poverty begins at the level of our identity, it creates a sense that, "This is just who I am. This is the way my life is." The word *poverty* in Scripture always has a possessive pronoun attached to it. Poverty is "theirs" in Proverbs 10:15, "yours" in Proverbs 24:34, and "his" in Proverbs 31:7. It seems strange that people would cling to ways of living that are self-inflicting, but that is the power of believing a lie.

Of course, the dark side of allowing lack to define your identity is that before long you are no longer the possessor, but the possessed. Our bent becomes our bondage (the word *bent* even derives from the Old English word meaning, "to put in bonds"). Charles Dickens gave us a colorful depiction of this in *A Christmas Carol*. When the ghost of Jacob Marley appears to his former partner, the miser Ebenezer Scrooge, he is bound with a chain:

> The chain he drew was clasped about his middle. It was long, and wound about him like a tail; and it was made (for Scrooge observed it closely) of cash-boxes, keys, padlocks, ledgers, deeds, and heavy purses wrought in steel.

When Scrooge asks him about it, Marley explains, "I wear the chain I forged in life. . . . I made it link by link, and yard by yard; I girded it on of my own free will, and of my own free will I wore it."[2]

Every one of us chooses bondage when we choose to listen to the lie of lack and let it define us, and this bondage is more than bad, destructive habits. When we listen to and believe lies, we empower the father of lies. Jesus called Satan by several names, one of which is "the father of lies." Another is Beelzebub,[3] meaning "Lord of Flies," and it contains a powerful picture. People in Jesus' day were well aware of flies and where they congregate: waste, death and wounds. Just as infection attracts flies, so the fear of lack attracts the harassment of evil spirits. It invites them to help make that fear our reality. Fear is faith in the negative.

We will never overcome the influence of Poverty until we learn to become stewards of what voices we listen to. This is why Jesus instructed us to be vigilant about our "hearing":

> "Take care what you listen to. By your standard of measure it will be measured to you; and more will be given you besides."
>
> Mark 4:24

Bill Johnson explains:

> Clearly Jesus is not referring merely to the physical act of perceiving sound. He's talking about hearing that involves listening. When we listen, we allow what we are hearing to gain our attention and focus, which in turn influences our beliefs and values. These beliefs and values set a standard for our ears that ultimately determines the voices that we pick up in our environment.[4]

If we allow the message of Poverty to set the standard for our ears, we will hear that message all around us. It is like tuning into a radio frequency. Francis Frangipane explains that a *power* (see Ephesians 6:12) is an evil energy that broadcasts lies like radio waves over a territory. For this reason, he says:

The means through which the church successfully wars against powers is through the administration of Christ's spiritual authority and the principle of displacement. Powers are not "cast out." They are displaced in the spirit-realm by the fullness of the reign of Christ in the church, and through the intercessory warfare of the saints in the region.[5]

Let's say the power of Poverty is a radio station that broadcasts the lie of lack. How do we retrain our thinking against these broadcasts? It isn't sufficient simply to tune the enemy out. We must choose to tune in to a different message; we need to change the channel. The only way to *unbend* our souls from a poverty paradigm is to *displace* the lie of lack by embracing the core message of the prosperous soul: There is always enough. In fact, there is always enough for *you*, because *you* are worthy in Christ. This message of abundance that "all things are yours" will establish your soul in your God-given identity and purpose. Ultimately, as the Church corporately embraces the message of abundance, we will become our own station for broadcasting this message to the world. We'll put the enemy out of business as we introduce everyone in our sphere of influence to the reality of heaven's economy.

Consider how renewing your mind with "there is always enough" displaces a Poverty spirit with a prosperous soul:

- Where a Poverty spirit creates anxiety, a prosperous soul is anxious for nothing. The threat of calamity fails to sway you, for you know that God will be faithful in all things. When He entrusts you with more, you know that He will also give you the grace to handle it well.
- Where a Poverty spirit hoards, a prosperous soul *conserves* and *uses*. You find creative and beneficial ways to recycle and reuse things.

- Where a Poverty spirit believes, "Things just happen to me," a prosperous soul believes, "I'm here to be a blessing." You dream of how you can best develop your passions and gifts to make the world better, and you gladly pay the price to do so.
- Where a Poverty spirit reaches for instant gratification, a prosperous soul exercises self-control toward goals and dreams. You take time to think and pray about the best that God has for you, and you budget according to those priorities.
- Where a Poverty spirit hounds you, a prosperous soul brings contentment. Even as you passionately run after the things God has put in your heart, you do so from a place of rest and gratitude, knowing that your source of happiness is not achievement but His abiding presence. You feel His favor on you, you know He is the ultimate prize and you know He will supply all your needs according to His riches in glory (see Philippians 4:19).
- Where a Poverty spirit feels out of control, a prosperous soul protects and delights in unlimited access to the strength and wisdom of God. Even in the midst of your mistakes, you know that if you seek Him, God will teach you and give you the ability to grow in mastering yourself and your resources.
- Where a Poverty spirit hides you, a prosperous soul is completely secure. You know you have the attention and favor of the God of the universe, and that when the time comes for you to speak up, He will give you words of wisdom and grace to help those who hear.
- Where a Poverty spirit chokes out generosity, a prosperous soul *revels* in it. You love to give! Practically nothing in the world makes you as happy as blessing someone else with the good things God has entrusted to you.

- Finally, where a Poverty spirit fights to keep you and others in the same condition, a prosperous soul seeks continual expansion and growth, and seeks always to empower and enrich others. You rejoice when others are blessed.

When you replace your poverty paradigm with a prosperity paradigm, your map of reality changes and expands. You see new bridges, roads and mountain passes. You see new lands and adventures. You see, in fact, that nothing is impossible. You see not bondage but unending freedom. The real voyage of a lifetime can finally begin.

But paradigm shifts are necessarily times of upheaval. They are uncomfortable. All our reference points for reality are thrown out of whack. As much as the message that "there is always enough" is biblical and therefore true, it is not going to *feel* true or *seem* true when we first start tuning in to it. We may be willing to turn ourselves over to God for a completely new mind, as painful as it may be, but for most of us it is something that ignites in us only when we're finally fed up with being lied to.

Consider Jacob. In Genesis 35:10, God changed his name to Israel: "God said to him, 'Your name is Jacob; you shall no longer be called Jacob, but Israel shall be your name.' Thus He called him Israel." It is fascinating to me that the name Jacob can mean "heel," "footprint" or "hind part."[6] And after Jacob wrestled with God, his name was changed to Israel, meaning "God strives"[7] or "to persist, to exert oneself, persevere."[8] Consider this interpretation: I believe Jacob wrestled with God to *displace* the power of lack in his life. His former name implied one left behind (he was a "heel-catcher" from the womb; he was born without the birthright; he suffered wrong under Laban; he developed a history of lying and being lied to). But Jacob prospered. What Esau despised (see Genesis 25:31–34), Jacob prized. When Laban deceived (see Genesis 29:25), Jacob persisted. When Jacob was alone with God (see Genesis 32:24–30), he wrestled and won. Jacob's renaming sealed the theme of his life: He was a living demonstration of the law of displacement. When this displacement was complete, he became Israel, an entirely different person, for the rest of his life.

Scripture tells us we are all sons and daughters of God, coheirs with Christ. We are part of the royal family of heaven. We already have a new name. The only problem is that we feel like imposters. And so we must wrestle with the truth of who God says we are until it becomes reality. And we must wrestle, like Jacob, as if our lives depend on it. For they do.

Where We Begin

Have you noticed that one of the bravest things you can do when you're afraid of something is just to admit it? Being honest is always courageous, even if you're being honest about your lack of courage. Significantly, learning to be prosperous begins in the same way. Jesus said "Blessed are the poor in spirit, for theirs is the kingdom of heaven" (Matthew 5:3).

Note how similar "poor in spirit" appears to be with "Poverty spirit." Yet there is one big difference between them. Both the poor in spirit and those with Poverty spirits know they lack, but only the first understands that this lack is spiritual. As a result, the one who is poor in spirit seeks the Father to be filled. Jacob is a great example of someone who was poor in spirit. By contrast, the one with a Poverty spirit is bound in fear; he thinks the lack is something temporal. Thus, he goes after more money, more friends, more power, more experiences and never recognizes his deep need for God.

The revelation given to the poor in spirit is the pivot point for those who would leave poverty for prosperity. The poor in spirit actually *subvert* the Poverty spirit by ceasing to fear lack and, instead, simply face it. The poor in spirit freely admit, "I am poor. I am needy. And I need *You*." Into such empty, open souls God has ever found a place to pour Himself out. Thus, to embrace our need is the foundational step in receiving a prosperous soul.

Of course, as they say, old habits die hard. Developing the kind of vulnerability and trust necessary to stand before God in desperate need, and then to receive His overwhelming abundance, is not something any of us can do well right away. Our old habits of hoarding, worrying, quitting and withholding simply have to die if we are ever to learn to do it well. Changing the channel sounds easy, and in one sense it is easy. In another sense, it takes unlearning the ways of Poverty and learning to live in prosperity. In the next chapter, we will dig into some of the nuts and bolts involved in this process.

Take a moment to consider the voices that claim your attention. Consider how you and others speak of their lives. Are the voices faith-filled and hopeful? Or are they pessimistic and discouraging? Write down some of your observations. How would you describe the standard you have set for your ears? Also, go back over the lists describing the qualities of the Poverty spirit and the prosperous soul. Make note of the things that seem most familiar to you. Do you recognize a "bent" toward "poverty thinking" in your life?

4

Trust and Faith

Either make the tree good and its fruit
good, or make the tree bad and its fruit
bad; for the tree is known by its fruit.

Matthew 12:33

Three small-town friends, brandishing newly adolescent bodies, blustered around the room in teen bravado. Boasting and speculating, their conversation swung from girls to sports and back to girls again.

One of the boys discovered his father's handgun in a desk drawer. It was a Saturday Night Special, a .38 caliber pistol, chrome with a pearl handle. The three studied the gun and began to work the mechanical slide, allowing the spring to recoil, feeling its sterile refinement, unaware they had levered into the firing chamber a single round from the magazine. They passed the gun between themselves, testing its weight and clicking the safety lock off and on.

The skinny kid began to wave the gun about. Squeezing the trigger, he yelled "bang" to imitate a shot, but was drowned out by a deafening boom from the barrel. The air was riven, wrenching the boys into a cruel reality. Two stood frozen in horror as the third boy, Tom, melted slowly to the floor, motionless and unnatural.

Seized by horror, shouts sounded like miniature voices in their ringing ears: "Tom, wake up!" In a blind panic, one boy exploded through the front door of the house, glancing off the mailbox, running to find help. The skinny kid who had fired the shot called 911, carefully relaying details as his mind numbed amid the chaos. He holstered the gun, and shock and guilt rose in his throat as he realized what had happened. How could it be he had unleashed such a terrible, fatal power on his gentle friend?

Police and paramedics arrived, awash in red and blue flashes, and whisked Tom to the hospital. Physicians and nurses worked frantically against the inevitable. Twelve hours passed.

Sitting in the waiting room, the skinny, small-town boy waited with friends and family for news. Resting his head in his hands, he groaned and cried, "What have I done?" Nothing could dislodge the bone of self-loathing trapped in his throat, nor could those sitting nearby bridge the gulf of his private misery. Lifting sodden eyes, he looked around the room and whispered softly, "I'm so sorry. Tom, I'm so sorry. Please, forgive me."

Suddenly, the room seemed to stretch before him like elastic. A haze came over everything. Wide-eyed, the boy scanned the faces of the others as if through a murky veil. The next moment, he heard a gentle voice ask, "Why?" Startled, the boy looked around. No one else had heard the voice. His head fell back into his hands. *Oh my God*, he thought, *I'm hearing things. I'm going insane.*

Patiently, the voice asked again, "Why?" Frightened by its nearness, the boy turned to try to see who had addressed him. Then a thought entered his mind: *Perhaps it's Tom! Perhaps he is asking me why I did it. This is my chance to explain, to ask forgiveness.* In the next few moments, the boy poured out his guilty heart to his friend, explaining and pleading. Hot tears, heavy with regret, cascaded down his face.

Then a miracle happened: Forgiveness entered the room. The heavy burden of sin and condemnation lifted from his narrow shoulders and dissolved like a specter. A few moments later, the haze dissipated and the room returned to its former dimensions. And in those moments, Tom slipped from his coma into eternity.

Taking Heaven by Force

I will forever hide the true names of these boys, save one. That skinny, small-town boy's name was Stephen De Silva. And this story represents a terrible but important chapter in my journey toward having a prosperous soul. My encounter in the "elastic room" actually happened. On that day, the weight of sin pressed on me like an invisible hand. I had pulled a trigger and hurled one beautiful friend into death, and another and myself into madness. As I came to realize later, it had not been Tom who had asked *why*, but the Holy Spirit. He had mercifully come to lead me out of the twisted forests of paralyzing condemnation. I cried out for forgiveness . . . and found it.

My forgiveness, along with the later knowledge that God had seen to Tom's salvation a mere thirty days before the accident, eased the grieving process. Still, it was very painful. I wrestled with all the difficult questions as to why such things happen. And, of course, I had to walk through the pain with

Tom's family and many others the accident had touched. Then there was the matter of moving forward in my life.

Life did move forward. I found faith in Jesus and increasingly flourished as I applied the Bible to my daily world. I was blessed with a beautiful wife and family. I worked hard and took my education into a job and then a career. Ten years after the accident, I was buying my second home and struggling to manage a small but growing measure of success.

Despite this outward growth, I began to recognize a quiet, internal discomfort with my life, and it involved finances. I was like most Americans; using my resources to realize the American dream meant taking on debt. I saw this as unavoidable, but also highly regrettable, as it seemed to prescribe a life of drudgery and grinding monotony. I managed to allay my feelings of dread with more hard work, discipline and various justifications for my financial choices, but the feelings never fully left me. Also, certain failures exacerbated my fear. My investments, though carefully designed, ended in losses; impulsive choices devoured my savings. These behaviors and circumstances seemed to repeat as cycles that led me, again and again, back into poverty and debt. My financial training and Bible study helped me identify these patterns as evidence of a Poverty spirit, but this knowledge didn't relieve my gnawing insecurity and discouragement.

The cycles became more pronounced as I grew older, as did my discomfort, which finally became unbearable. It seemed as though I were two different people. My life had many signs of success: I was a faithful husband and father, capable of meaningful connections with friends, skillful in managing my business, courageous when contending for justice and truth. At the same time, my fear and discouragement over debt and failures persisted. And the persistence of these feelings began to clue me in to their extensive root system in my soul—a system of deep-seated negative feelings and beliefs about myself.

Like Jacob in his years of servitude to his father-in-law, I was both blessed and oppressed. And, like Jacob, I finally realized I had to do something to break free from the destructive cycles in my life. But I understood, as Jesus said, that I couldn't make the fruit of my life good without making the whole tree good. And I could never make the tree of my life good, which is why I needed Christ. But I didn't have a living awareness of it. I had to get to the roots; I had to work with Christ at the foundations of my being hidden deep in my soul.

The hard reality about repairing foundations is that you have to stop building on top of them. In fact, often you have to tear down what you've built in order to locate faults and make repairs. Thus I found myself, middle-aged and tired, faced with the question: Was I willing to tear down in order to build better and higher? Counting the cost, I decided the pain of staying where I was outweighed the pain of facing my fears and making radical changes in my life. I also decided I would not settle for less than complete and total restoration of my heart and soul. I resorted to spiritual violence: "The kingdom of heaven suffers violence, and violent men take it by force" (Matthew 11:12).

Pushing past the urge to protect myself from pain, I determined to *take heaven by force* and prevail in my own healing. I scheduled a Sozo session (the inner healing ministry I described in chapter 1). I had undergone a session before, but this time I had a particular enemy in the "crosshairs" of my holy intentions. I augmented this by seeking paid professional counseling from an anointed Christian marriage and family counselor. I also scheduled meetings with loving mentors and counselors who gave honest feedback. I sought out the prophetic ministry in our church. I frequented the Alabaster House, the prayer chapel at Bethel Church, and spent many aggressive hours in prayer, allowing the Holy Spirit to plumb the deep places of my heart. I continued for months with no thought of wavering. God was real. He would repair my cracked foundations.

Trust Is the Foundation

Through this season of healing, I learned much about how God designed us as creatures of *trust*. In his theory of psychosocial development, sociologist Erik Erikson posits that trust is the first, and thus foundational, developmental task for human beings. Upon this foundation we build our identities, learn what is possible and develop relationships.[1] However, the reality of living in a fallen world is that we inhabit a world where trust is broken—with ourselves, with each other and most deeply with God. It was a breach of trust that brought sin, and all that has come of it, into the world. Thus, the heart of God's plan for healing the world of sin is not only to forgive us, but also to restore our trust—and, through restoring our trust, to restore all that we are.

Perhaps you're familiar with the old story of the brave acrobat who claimed he could tightrope walk over Niagara Falls. A crowd gathered to watch the daring feat. Carefully, the acrobat climbed onto the tightrope, walked out over the falls, turned and walked back to the solid riverbank. Next, he made the journey while pushing a wheelbarrow. For the final trip, he asked a reporter in the crowd if he would like to ride inside the wheelbarrow as the acrobat pushed it along the tightrope above the falls. Promptly, the reporter replied, "No sir!" Surprised, the acrobat asked whether he believed he could do it. The reporter replied, "Yes, I believe you can do it. I just don't trust you."[2]

Believing that God can do something is different from trusting Him to do it. Trust gets us into the wheelbarrow; it is an action that commits us to risk. And because it is an action, it can only be done in the present. It's easy to think we're trusting God when we apply what He says only to the past or the future. But it's only in the present moment that we can truly trust God. And God, like the acrobat, keeps inviting us beyond the passive watching of what He can do and into joining Him in what He is doing. This persistent call exposes our lack of trust and brings us to the point of decision.

One day during my season of restoration, I had a "wheelbarrow" experience in our church's prayer chapel. In my spirit, I heard God tell me I was lovely. I promptly thanked Him, shrugging off the compliment as something normal for the Creator to say to His creation. Then He spoke again: "You are significant." I was confused by this, but I knew God was up to something with me. I asked Him why He had said this. In response, He told me to say aloud, "I am significant." *Okay,* I thought, *that's easy enough.* "I am siggg. I am signifff. I. I . . . I." I could not force the words out of my mouth.

God's instruction had put a finger directly on what I honestly thought of myself. As I meditated on this, I saw a picture of myself as a large pipe. I believed God was willing to use me, in spite of myself, as a pipe to carry His beauty and goodness whenever I served and lived "like a Christian." But God was asking me if I saw the pipe as good in itself—and I did not. I also knew that because He had said this about me—that I was significant—this truth had to become my reality.

I left the chapel with a challenge from the Lord that required my active trust. I was to practice saying, "I am significant," until I could say it and mean it. It literally took me days to say it. Then I had to say it to my wife. Then to my friends. Then to my class! As I practiced declaring this simple revelation over my life, it began a deep revolution in my thinking about the most basic tenets of the Gospel: salvation, redemption and forgiveness. I learned that Christ's work on the cross was so true and effective that it even makes the pipe lovely. My belief in my insignificance had been a denial of the work of the cross, from which I had to repent. After a few weeks of obeying the Lord and renewing my mind, I had a breakthrough. I could say the phrase, "I am significant," and mean it. It had begun to be my reality.

My deepening knowledge of salvation, forgiveness and my significance in God's eyes peeled more layers, like an onion, off my memories of the shooting accident. Sometime during this process, I eventually located some of the deepest roots of my negative feelings in these memories. This was somewhat surprising to me, as I had unmistakably received forgiveness for the accident, and could think of it without any feelings of condemnation. I knew God would never punish me for what I had done. However, I discovered that this event had left a profound mark on my forming teenage identity. I knew I had been forgiven enough not to be punished, but I didn't know I had been forgiven enough to make me a person of value, a person worth trusting. And I had believed the opposite.

Oysters and Pearls

My trust in this lie created a "bent" in my soul, a pattern of thinking, feeling and choosing that defined my reality for years. Though such patterns often begin from a single experience, like my shooting accident, they gather momentum by positioning us to experience other things in the same way. Thus, for example, an experience of unkind words or neglect leads a young girl to trust in the lie that she isn't beautiful. This creates a pattern that sets her up to experience the message again and again until it becomes her reality. This process is like an oyster forming a pearl around a grain of sand. It is strange we can treat such destructive lies like treasures, enshrining them as our personal truths ever more permanently with each layer of experience. But we do, as we see most clearly when Christ comes with the truth that we are beautiful or significant. He exposes just how much we have treasured beliefs to the contrary—even though they have made us miserable!

Jesus described His Kingdom reality as the "pearl of great value" (Matthew 13:46). His treasure exposes our false treasure for what it really is. And His call to greatness makes us dissatisfied and hopeful to break from the destructive cycles that so many around us accept as "normal"—the cycles created as we keep building our lives on the flawed foundation of trust in lies. Above all, His truth continues to draw us away from these false realities and into His reality.

Truth is always more powerful than lies, though it does take time for truth's power to do its work in us. Jesus said the reality of the Kingdom is like leaven, hidden inside us and gradually permeating our being (see Luke 13:20–21). The reality of my forgiveness from Him—which not only freed me from guilt and punishment but also restored me as a son of God—began working in me from the moment I put my trust in Christ. This meant the lies of unworthiness, fear and mistrust (the roots of the Poverty spirit) I had believed were ultimately bound to come under direct fire by the truth: *I had been reconciled to God and made worthy in Christ* (the roots of the prosperous soul). It was God "at work in [me], both to will and to work for His good pleasure" that finally provoked me to take heaven by force and to "work out [my] salvation" more thoroughly in my soul (Philippians 2:13, 12).

Paul tells us God is working to transform us "from glory to glory" (2 Corinthians 3:18). A few verses later he says that the "momentary, light affliction" involved in this transformation process "is producing for us an eternal *weight of glory* far beyond all comparison" (2 Corinthians 4:17, emphasis mine). As God takes us from glory to glory, He is adding weight to our lives. This truth enabled me to see that the increasing *mass* of spiritual substance and its accelerating momentum in my life was bringing my character under greater "stress tests"—and it eventually exposed the flaws in my trust. The prosperous soul that Christ was establishing in me could not remain within the narrow confines created by my insecurity and low self-worth. Neither could my flawed foundation support the weight of influence, authority and wealth—the weight of a greater glory—that accompanied this prosperous soul.

Many Christians have not yet learned to trust in God's goodness and love. And so they mistakenly think the exposure of their character flaws is proof that their salvation isn't working. The exact opposite is true! The true work of grace and glory in your life is to bring everything into the light so you can see the broken places, invite God's healing and gain wisdom and strength to live differently. God doesn't want to take you down; He wants to take you higher. Understanding this will free you forever from discouragement and condemnation!

Stewardship

Every passage of Scripture on stewardship in the New Testament deals with the issue of trust. The message on this subject is clear: *Stewardship is a trust.* The more God adds to our lives, the more He is trusting us. Again, stewardship, as with all God calls us to, is about *partnership*. And because God wants partners who are *like Him*, He never calls us to do something without showing us how to do it Himself. God didn't simply ask me to trust Him; He trusted me, and His trust ultimately exposed my lack of trust in Him and in who He says I am. Yet it was also His trust in me that taught me how to begin to trust both Him and myself—in short, to start thinking and acting like the son and supernatural steward He was training me to be.

Our stewardship of money exposes the state of our trust as nothing else does. This is why God continues to use money, like the master in the parable of the talents, to identify His "good and faithful servants." As I said before, money is power, and power exaggerates whatever is in our hearts, which is what God is most interested in. He doesn't need us to make money for Him, and it doesn't cost Him to give us more. But it cost Him His own Son to restore us as sons and daughters who could share in His glory and Kingdom. Only faithful and trusting hearts can bear the weight of that glory. This is why the most prized quality of the steward is not financial acumen, nor hard work, nor even courage to take risks—but *faithfulness* and *trustworthiness*. "It is required of stewards that one be found trustworthy" (1 Corinthians 4:2).

Jesus taught that the quality of our faithfulness can be seen in our lives, no matter how small or great the issue at stake:

> He who is faithful in a very little thing is faithful also in much; and he who is unrighteous in a very little thing is unrighteous also in much.
>
> Luke 16:10

The Lord is also the only One who can finally answer the question of whether or not we are being faithful—to no other person will we give an account of how we have stewarded our lives. Moreover, He is the only One who enables us to be faithful, as Paul taught:

> Who are you to judge the servant of another? To his own master he stands or falls; and he will stand, for the Lord is able to make him stand.
>
> Romans 14:4

Still, we are to look for specific evidence of faithfulness in ourselves and in the Body of Christ. Christ said, "You will know them by their fruits" (Matthew 7:20). And He demonstrated the kind of fruit we're to look for: that of a life lived from perfect trust in God. Christ modeled the standard of faithfulness to which we all must aspire, and is thus the prime example of a *believer* (which we do well to remember when we use this term to describe ourselves). He declared:

> "These signs will follow those who believe: In My name they will cast out demons; they will speak with new tongues; they will take up serpents; and if they drink anything deadly, it will by no means hurt them; they will lay hands on the sick, and they will recover."
>
> Mark 16:17–18, NKJV

Notice that all of these "signs following" involve actions— and not passive actions, but aggressive, offensive acts against evil. Real trust in a supernatural God will manifest in this kind of supernatural behavior—Christ-like behavior. When I consider Christ's lifestyle, it strikes me that no one could describe the "signs that followed" Christ with words like *conservative* or *careful*. Yes, He did instruct His disciples to pick up the leftovers after He multiplied the loaves and fishes. But such "conservation" only serves to point out that Christ ministered from extravagant generosity and abundance! This is the kind of supernatural stewardship that flows from a heart that trusts God completely and knows what God is truly like.

If we say we believe but can't identify this kind of behavior in our lives ("signs that follow"), our *belief* may not be genuine *trust* in God. We can locate what we truly trust by examining our behavior. Consider: What are some of the "signs that follow" you, and what do they point to? What are some of the signs of genuine trust that are missing from your life?

Breaking Trust with Lies

Trust is the bedrock of the prosperous soul. Isaiah 26:3 says, "You will keep in perfect peace him whose mind is steadfast [stayed on you], because he trusts in you" (NIV). "Perfect peace" is perhaps the best that English can do in two words to capture the meaning of *shalom*. *Shalom* is one of the most lavish words in existence. It *is* richness, prosperity, wholeness, health and safety. There is no better word to describe the quality of a prosperous soul. And God keeps you in *shalom* when your "mind is stayed" on Him. This literally means that *the entire framework of your thinking rests upon God.*

There is no trusting God, and consequently no prosperity of soul, without allowing Him to rewire our thinking with His truth. But as He does reveal the truth, it will not lead us into *shalom* unless we "get in the wheelbarrow." As Christ taught:

> "Everyone who hears these words of Mine *and acts upon them*, may be compared to a wise man who built his house on rock. And the rain fell, and the floods came, and the winds blew and slammed against that house; and yet it did not fall, for it had been founded on the rock. Everyone who hears these

words of Mine *and does not act on them*, will be like a foolish man who built his house on the sand. The rain fell, and the floods came, and the winds blew and slammed against that house; and it fell—and great was its fall."

Matthew 7:24–27, emphasis mine

According to Jesus, our foundation of trust will be healed and made firm as we *hear* the Lord's words and then *act* on them. As I discovered, one of the most powerful ways to start acting is to use *our* words. I have experienced the truth of what other Christian teachers have said: Nothing happens in the Kingdom of heaven unless there is first a declaration. With this principle in mind, the following section contains a series of prayers and declarations developed over time in my Prosperous Soul class.

Prayers and Declarations

The following prayers and declarations make room for the Holy Spirit to put His finger on any lies you may be trusting. They also give you the opportunity to repent and establish your trust in truth.

First, I invite you to pray the following prayer:

Father God, I am Your child. I gave my life to You on _____ (name the date or period of your commitment to Christ). You have proven Your faithful goodness to generations before me. And You will again show Your goodness to me right now. I need Your grace to discover the lies I have trusted, and I ask You now to show them to me.

Spend a few moments listening for whatever God would reveal. Below are many of the lies that my students have bravely and honestly identified in their thinking (the list is actually several pages long). I hope that reading these will be helpful to you.

Lies of Fear

- Something has to go wrong, because I'm feeling way too good.
- I am afraid for my future because of all my past mistakes.
- I am too much trouble, and not enough "good."
- I'm afraid of failure.
- I'm afraid of success.

Lies of Shame and Worthlessness

- What I think doesn't matter.
- I am worthless.
- I am incapable of stewarding money well.
- I am weak because of my failures.
- I need to keep up appearances so rich people will think well of me.
- I don't deserve love, money or health.
- I'm just a _____ (mechanic, teacher, clerk, etc.).
- I will always be the poor one in the family.
- I don't deserve to be wealthy because I haven't been good enough with money.
- What I want is too much to ask for.
- I am stupid.
- God is too big and too busy to pay attention to me.
- My family is cursed.
- Negative thoughts are part of who I am.

- God isn't big enough to deal with my problems and free me completely.
- God won't prosper me because of my mistakes.
- I haven't done enough to earn blessings or favor.
- I have to somehow earn my right to prosper.

Lies of Hopelessness

- I will never be free of sin.
- I'm not creative.
- My family doesn't expect me ever to prosper.
- I'm destined to be poor.
- Because of my age I am overlooked.
- Younger (or older, more experienced) people will be chosen over me.
- I will be dependent on my children because of lost money.
- I'll never truly thrive.
- I will never get out from under the weight of my debt.
- Things and problems in my life will never change.
- I have no one to leave an inheritance to, so why should I bother?

Lies about Money

- The rich are unhappy.
- You have to have money to get money.
- Money diverts you from the Kingdom.
- Wealth equals evil.
- Money controls you.
- You can't follow the Lord and have money, too.

- It's too much work to make money.
- If I make money, I'll forget my dependence on God.

This list is not exhaustive or authoritative, but it serves to reveal something significant: Most of these lies are associated with wounds that have trained us to trust in distortions regarding *God's provision* and our *God-given identity*. These two areas are the core of both the Poverty and the prosperity message. We are either living as sons and daughters, secure that "all things are ours" and that nothing is impossible—or we are living in fear of lack, feeling distant from God and feeling powerless to change ourselves and our circumstances. These are the two primary "programs" that run in our thinking and behavior. (There is a third, which you will see in the chapter on Mammon.) The Poverty program is all too familiar for most of us, and it is what kicks in when we go on autopilot. We must be violent in taking heaven by force and challenging our thinking and behavior with the truth of prosperity. Begin to strike at the roots of that old programming with this prayer:

> Father God, I recognize that these lies create destructive forces in my life. I recognize that You did not teach me these things, but I have learned them from people and events in my past.
>
> I forgive those people now. I forgive _____ (quietly speak their names as God brings them to your mind) and release him/her into Your hand.
>
> I forsake those events now. I forgive myself for _____ (quietly renounce events in your past as God brings them to your mind) and release those into Your hand.
>
> I ask you, Father, to strike these lies at the root and sever their effect in my life, my family's history and my family's future.
>
> Finally, Father, I ask You to replace each of these lies with biblical truth. Occupy my heart with Your Word. Improve my soil and bless my destiny as a prosperous soul. Bless my family tree with abundant life. Amen.

Now, as a prophetic act, take out two pieces of paper. On one, write down the lies that the Holy Spirit reveals to you. On the other, write down the truth that God reveals. For each lie, repeat this prayer:

> I sever, by faith in Jesus Christ, the root lie of _____ right now. (Repeat this prayer for every lie God has shown you. Continue until every one has been addressed.)

When you are finished, physically destroy the first paper and make this declaration over yourself: "I am a prosperous soul." Keep the second paper of truths somewhere convenient, and continue to add your discoveries as you proceed with God. Invite God to show you practical ways to trust these truths, to "get into the wheelbarrow" and act on them until they become your reality. And look for the supernatural signs that follow.

Finally, remember you'll never change the "fruit" of your life and behavior without addressing the "roots" of trust in your heart and soul. Every time the Lord graciously convicts you about your behavior, don't waste your energy trying to "pick" the fruit and control how things appear on the outside. Instead, ask Him to "make the tree good" by showing you how to break your trust in a lie and establish your trust in Him. In the spirit, as in nature, until you sever the root, you will not change the fruit.

5

Dreaming

They said to one another, "Here comes this dreamer!"

Genesis 37:19

Our Dreams Matter

I believe that God engineered each of us to *dream*—to envision the fulfillment of our hopes and desires. In fact, dreaming is so vital for us that without it, none of us will reach our full potential in life. A dream is like a buoy that lifts us above mediocrity and monotony. Yet even more fundamentally, dreaming keeps us *alive,* because it connects us to *vision.* The Bible says that without vision a person will "let go": "Where there is no vision, the people are unrestrained" (Proverbs 29:18).

The New American Standard Bible translates the Hebrew word *para* (meaning to "let go" or "neglect") as "unrestrained." Other translations of this verse choose "perish."

The final result of being unrestrained is that we perish, and it all happens through lack of vision.

In his marvelous book *Blood River: A Journey to Africa's Broken Heart*, British author Tim Butcher describes his heroic journey retracing the Congo River journey of explorer Henry Morton Stanley, who was famous for the phrase, "Dr. Livingstone, I presume?" Sir Stanley's adventure on one of the world's great rivers began in 1871, and Butcher followed the same path 130 years later. In the intervening century, the vast nation of Congo had weathered the devastating effects of the slave trade, colonization and vicious despotism under President Mobutu, which led to the deaths of millions of Congolese people. As the title of Butcher's book suggests, the economic and social atrocities left Congo morally and fiscally devastated.

I was appalled as Butcher described the country's utter lack of hope. Congo is a demonstration on a national scale of the consequences that come upon a people who have lost their vision and are perishing for it. Historically, societies have been constructed to provide communities with commerce and safety. Not so in Congo. The wild jungle provides safety, while most towns are under constant threat from marauders and murderous vigilantes. Congo is a dreamless nation, standing as an emblem of governmental corruption and economic devolution.[1]

Sadly, places like Congo provide some of the clearest evidence that we *need* to dream. With a dream, humankind's potential for greatness, justice and beauty are on display. Without it, we are left to experience the worst that humankind can offer.

Why Do We Stop Dreaming?

Because each of us is born with the capacity and need to dream, the question arises: Why do we stop dreaming? And when? What causes us to stop?

I have asked these questions in my Prosperous Soul class and people are quick to give responses. It is from this living survey that I have gathered the most common reasons into three categories:

"I am too busy to dream."
"I am too afraid to dream."
"I am too wounded to dream."

I want to address each of these in this chapter.

"I am too busy to dream."

I understand *busy*. One day, I found myself nine years deep into a seven-day work schedule. I'm not sure how I got there, except by good intentions and an overdeveloped sense of self-importance. I came by these traits honestly—working long and hard every day was the way of life on the cattle ranch where I grew up. My family fed the livestock, cut, raked and hauled hay, and we fell into bed exhausted every night. Each hard day's work promised a payday sometime in the future, when we sold the hay and the cattle at auction. I carried this work ethic through college, through my early years working for various accounting firms, and finally to Bethel Church. When I needed to supplement my Bethel income, I opened an income tax and consulting practice, which I maintained by working on evenings and weekends.

I worked for Bethel and ran my business every day for nine years. Then one night, Someone disturbed my sleep. At 2:30 A.M., probably while snoring softly beside my wife, I had a remarkable dream. I can still remember it clearly: I was seated in my office at Bethel, typing at my computer and cradling a telephone between my shoulder and chin. As I simultaneously conversed with someone on the phone and typed on the spreadsheet before me, another person came to my office door with a question. Turning, I nodded a response, not losing pace with either the person on the phone or my place on the spreadsheet.

As often happens in dreams, I stood outside myself, watching the scene play out. Beside me was Father God, who was there, I thought, to watch my impressive display of efficiency. I turned from watching my busy self and smiled at the Lord, as if to ask, *I'm doing well, eh, Papa?*

"This is not from Me," was His calm reply.

Lurching awake from this vivid dream, my blood ran cold. If my busy life wasn't from God, who was it from? I knew overwork originating from my own flesh or the outside pressure of the world could be solved easily enough by studying Stephen Covey's 7 *Habits of Highly Effective People.* But something told me there was more to this dream. What if my frantic existence had been *given* to me? My mind raced with questions as I heard this phrase repeat over and over: "Evil one . . . evil one." Unable to sleep, I found a Bible and turned to the only verse I remembered with that phrase:

> We know that we are of God, and that the whole world lies in the power of the evil one.
>
> 1 John 5:19

Using my *Strong's Concordance*, I learned that "evil one" in this verse means "to toil." Sensing that I had found the beginning pieces for solving this puzzle, I scribbled some notes on a page, made my way back to bed and quickly fell asleep.

The next morning, I spent time praying, asking God what I was to make of the dream and pondering the meaning of "evil one" in 1 John 5:19. I continued deeper into the meaning of "evil one" with my Bible software. I found the phrase is used ten times in the New American Standard translation, all of which are in the New Testament. I then read the ten verses, and now, with my new knowledge of the word's definition, they sounded completely different to me. Consider these ten verses when "evil one" is replaced with "toil":

When anyone hears the word of the kingdom and does not understand it, *toil* comes and snatches away what has been sown in his heart. This is the one on whom seed was sown beside the road.

Matthew 13:19

And the field is the world; and as for the good seed, these are the sons of the kingdom; and the tares are the sons of *toil*.

Matthew 13:38

I do not ask You to take them out of the world, but to keep them from *toil*.

John 17:15

In addition to all, taking up the shield of faith with which you will be able to extinguish all the flaming arrows of *toil*.

Ephesians 6:16

But the Lord is faithful, and He will strengthen and protect you from *toil*.

2 Thessalonians 3:3

I am writing to you, fathers, because you know Him who has been from the beginning. I am writing to you, young men, because you have overcome *toil*. I have written to you, children, because you know the Father.

1 John 2:13

I have written to you, fathers, because you know Him who has been from the beginning. I have written to you, young men, because you are strong, and the word of God abides in you, and you have overcome *toil*.

1 John 2:14

Not as Cain, who was of *toil* and slew his brother. And for what reason did he slay him? Because his deeds were evil, and his brother's were righteous.

1 John 3:12

We know that no one who is born of God sins; but He who was born of God keeps him, and *toil* does not touch him.

1 John 5:18

We know that we are of God, and that the whole world lies in the power of *toil*.

1 John 5:19

As is clear in these verses, *toil* is not the same thing as *work*. Scripture repeatedly affirms the value of work, but always within the larger context of worship and service to God, in which our priority is relationship with Him. *Toil* means "to work extremely hard or incessantly"; it derives from a verb meaning "to drag, struggle."[2] Toil is an oppressive spiritual force that, among other things, separates work from its spiritual purpose and drives away the other vital activities necessary for maintaining our connection with God's presence. It is easy to come under the influence of toil by mistakenly thinking, as I did, that busyness for a noble or spiritual cause is pleasing to God. But God was not impressed with my toil because it kept me from my relationship with Him. After persisting in my studies, the Holy Spirit again spoke to me, with these three short words: "Keep My Sabbath."

His answer to my problem of busyness was different from simply "stop doing that." As everything God says is deeper than it first appears, so Sabbath is not an arbitrary test of obedience. It is a revelation of His design and purpose for success in life. When we try to live outside His design, it causes problems. But in order to live in His design, we must trust His revelation and instruction above our own ideas. In my case, keeping the Sabbath meant dropping from my schedule a productive day—a day that, in fact, accounted for roughly 30 percent of my private accounting business. By any human account, cutting a third of your productivity is not a wise business strategy. Though I knew I could trust God's instruction, it still took a tremendous effort of faith from me to begin devoting an entire day to practicing rest. (Anyone under the influence of toil knows it takes more faith to rest than to stay busy!)

As we read in Ephesians 6:16, faith is a shield that has the capacity to protect us from the influence of toil in our lives. When I began taking up the shield of faith through keeping the Sabbath, I got a revelation of what I hadn't been protecting by keeping up my busy lifestyle: my ability to dream. Toil had crowded out my dreams, along with other things that require leisure time, things such as studying, meditating, creating and playing. God wanted to restore these things in my life, because they are vital to developing a prosperous soul.

The more I experience the benefits of keeping the Sabbath, the more clearly I see that many of us are missing out on these benefits. We live in a day of irony, in which our society has more labor-saving options available than ever, yet embraces a culture of jet-setting, multitasking, hyper-speed busyness. In fact, we have embraced slavery under toil. Not surprisingly, this slavery is linked to our slavery to debt, for our financial obligations demand that we work under toil. Keeping the Sabbath is an essential key for us to practice and preserve our freedom and resist slavery.

God prescribed the Sabbath for Israel immediately after freeing them from slavery in Egypt. Historian Thomas Cahill describes the connection between freedom and the Sabbath:

> No ancient society before the Jews had a day of rest. The God who made the universe and rested bids us to do the same, calling us to a weekly restoration of prayer, study, and recreation (or re-creation). In this study (or talmud), we have the beginnings of what Nahum Sarna has called "the universal duty of continual self-education," Israel being the first human society to so value education and the first to envision it as a universal pursuit—and a democratic obligation that those in power must safeguard on behalf of those in their employ. The connections to both freedom and creativity lie just below the surface of this commandment: leisure is appropriate to a free people, and this people so recently free find themselves quickly establishing this quiet weekly celebration of their freedom; *leisure is the necessary ground of creativity, and a free people are free to imitate the creativity of God.* The Sabbath is surely one of the simplest and sanest recommendations any god has ever made; and those who live without such septimanal punctuation are emptier and less resourceful (emphasis mine).[3]

Leisure, as celebrated on the Sabbath, is conducive to freedom. And freedom is necessary to the dream. Without the dream, our creativity, by which we bring solutions, beauty and all else that makes our world better, is shut down. It is time for the Body of Christ to take up the shield of faith against the influence of toil, establish Sabbath rest in our lives and allow God to restore our dreams.

"I am too afraid to dream."

Another corrosive agent to our ability to dream is *fear.* The Bible says that perfect love casts out fear (see 1 John 4:18).

A corollary to this is that when we experience things that communicate anything less than perfect love to us, fear has the opportunity to seep into our hearts and minds.

One of the primary ways fear takes root in our lives is through loss. Many of us have had dreams stolen by circumstances beyond our control (or persons out of control). Other losses have been self-inflicted, leading many of us to believe we no longer deserve our dreams. We may recover to a point, but fear convinces us that dreaming is perilous, that it is safer to live without hope or expectation than to risk the loss of something we hold dear.

I had a childhood dream that was stolen years ago. This dream began for me as a young boy watching television on Sunday evenings. Though it was a school night, my parents let me stay up till 9 P.M. so I could finish watching *The Undersea World of Jacques Cousteau*. Each week I sat mesmerized by Mr. Cousteau's heavy French accent as he narrated his explorations of the mysteries of the deep. I imagined myself among his band of divers slipping beneath the turbulent ocean waves. I pretended I swam beside them, holding my breath behind puffed-out cheeks as long as I could. I carried a secret dream of becoming an oceanographer like my hero, Jacques Cousteau.

During high school, books and brochures on oceanography were irresistible to me. By that age, I had become a strong swimmer and had memorized every story my father had told me about his scuba adventures. After patiently waiting for many years, I enrolled in a class to train me in scuba diving. I signed up and devoured the course materials, happily memorizing dive charts, atmospheres and safety routines. The class practiced in a swimming pool. Suiting up, handling the equipment, submerging and feeling the thrill of a deep inhalation while underwater was all I had expected and more.

I was strong and naturally comfortable under the surface, moving easily and confidently among my classmates.

Eventually, the day arrived for our open-water test. Passing this final exam would earn me my dive certification and grant me the freedom I had dreamed of since childhood. My classmates, instructors and I suited up and waddled to the water's edge. We tested our equipment and double-checked one another for safety, as we had been drilled from the beginning. Finally, we all entered the water and . . . it was magical.

During the exam, we practiced basics such as inflating and deflating our buoyancy compensator so we could find weightlessness at various depths. We practiced navigating by compass so we could rely on a handheld instrument when visibility was poor. We exchanged masks, purged water from our air supply and learned to trust our dive partners in dangerous conditions.

We were underwater for nearly an hour, and after all these drills the final exercise came. The entire class slowly dropped to a depth of sixty feet and held a conversation with sign language. It all passed without incident, and when we were finished, the instructor signaled for us to ascend. As we slowly rose, I felt a strange discomfort grow in my chest. I tried to adjust my wetsuit but the feeling didn't leave. The higher I rose, the greater the discomfort grew. By the time I reached the surface, I felt as if a strong belt had tightened around my chest, preventing me from taking a deep breath. I wasn't in pain, but something was wrong.

I mentioned it to my instructor, and he helped me get over to shore and get my gear off. He checked me out but couldn't detect anything serious. He decided to accompany me to lunch, however, to make sure I was well. And I was well, except for this persistent, strange pressure in my chest. I finally decided to drive home and lie down for a while. I sat down in my lounge chair at home and reclined to take a nap, but as I lay my body back, I felt what can only be described as a *bubble* rumbling under my collarbone. It moved downward through my ribs to my abdomen. At that moment I experienced the worst pain of my life. I cried out in pain and returned to an upright position in a panic. The bubble moved again, seeming to rip out a new internal path as it returned to its former place under my collarbone.

Several hours later, I was gazing at the shadowy outlines of an X-ray film. The emergency room doctor explained I had suffered a pneumothorax, a condition experienced when the tissue of the lung is breached, leaking air into the sensitive area between the chest cavity and the lungs. When I lay flat, the bubble of air sought a higher spot, like the bubble in a carpenter's level. The searing pain was caused by delicate tissues being pulled apart as the bubble jiggled and forced its way around my tender insides.

Eventually, I recovered without treatment, as the air leached naturally into my body and disappeared after the punctured lung healed. But through this ordeal, I learned I had a physical condition on the surface of my lungs called *blebs*, which are essentially blisters, or weak spots, in the lung wall. Many people have this defect without ever knowing it. My problem was if I continued to dive, it would inevitably lead to a reoccurrence of a pneumothorax. I was given a 50 percent chance of dying from a heart attack if this were to happen again during a deep scuba dive. I realized that my dream and Jacques Cousteau's underwater world were forever out of my reach.

The disappointment clung to me for years. Eventually, I began to look for other sports or activities to pursue, but none satisfied the void left by my dashed underwater dream. In truth, I was afraid to open my heart to a new passion only to be disappointed again. I was afraid to dream.

As I journeyed further down the path of the prosperous soul and supernatural stewardship, my fear was confronted by the story of Joseph, one of the greatest dreamers in Scripture. As I have mentioned, Joseph's dreaming was critical to his success in weathering the difficulties that ultimately trained him to carry a stewardship strategy for saving a nation. But if anyone could have been intimidated out of his dream by loss—as well as hatred, kidnapping, abandonment, enslavement, harassment and imprisonment—it was Joseph.

Many who read Joseph's story conclude that his boldness to own and declare his dream caused him to suffer. But I believe the attacks on Joseph by his brothers and Potiphar's wife— and even the neglect of Pharaoh's cupbearer—were provoked by a Poverty spirit residing in those people. The true effect of Joseph's dream was that of a light exposing the Poverty spirit in others, inciting backlash of the worst kind.

We risk such effects when we dream, which is why dreaming—like love, trust and everything else that matters—requires great courage. Joseph's courage and integrity are clearly seen in his faithfulness to carry his dream through thirteen years of struggle and opposition. But this particular dream, because it was God-given and an expression of Joseph's divine purpose, gave to him as much as he gave to it. This is why we can recognize the outline of the dream in every circumstance Joseph faced. In his family, in prison and in the palace, Joseph found others "bowing to him" as he was favored. Because he was faithful to carry the dream, it faithfully carried him like a buoy to its fulfillment.

Joseph's life helped me to see the connection between dreaming and purpose. And I recognized that the fulfillment I had been seeking in my underwater dream did not lie in diving, or in any particular activity in itself, but rather in the expression of my purpose. Purpose is a gift from our

Creator; you could say that our purpose is *God's dream* for our lives. If we cling to the buoy of our divine purpose, we will find that we do not merely have a dream, or a few dreams, but that we awaken to new dreams in every season of our lives.

Pursuing my purpose led me to explore other areas of interest, believing that God had new dreams for me. By not giving up, and through experimentation, I eventually discovered a new and stronger passion than before. Now I teach, "Don't confuse the plan with your purpose." Most of the things we call our dreams are simply the manifold ways we express the core of who we are. A plan can be dashed by circumstances, timing or lack of resources, but purpose cannot. If your dream can be dashed, it is because you haven't reached high enough; you have mistaken a plan for your purpose.

Wonderfully, the more we come to know and understand our purpose, the less potential our disappointments have to intimidate us from dreaming. In the light of eternity, loss and difficulties take on their true significance: as tools in the hand of a God who "causes all things to work together for good to those who love God, to those who are called according to His purpose" (Romans 8:28). When we understand that nothing can diminish our purpose, nothing will have the power to derail us from walking in that purpose unless we allow it to do so.

I challenge you, if you have allowed yourself to be intimidated out of dreaming through an experience of loss or failure, take time to seek out the truth of your divine purpose more deeply. Open your heart to the God who wants to do "far more abundantly beyond all that [you] ask or think" (Ephesians 3:20). Invite Him to awaken your dreams again— and your courage to dream.

"*I am too wounded to dream.*"

The final enemy of the dream is hopelessness. "I'm too wounded to dream" are words of defeat. Instead, we are called to be victors—all of us.

> I saw something like a sea of glass mixed with fire, and those who had been *victorious* over the beast and his image and the number of his name, standing on the sea of glass, holding harps of God.
>
> Revelation 15:2, emphasis mine

> In all these things we overwhelmingly conquer through Him who loved us.
>
> Romans 8:37

Scripture is filled with exhortations to be strong and courageous and never to quit, and to do so for one reason: God is with us. As long as we stay with Him, we are guaranteed success.

Hopelessness is a state that is completely out of character for a believer, because the believer's soul is *anchored in hope*:

> We desire that each one of you *show the same diligence so as to realize the full assurance of hope* until the end, so that you will not be sluggish, but imitators of those who through faith and patience inherit the promises. For when God made the promise to Abraham, since He could swear by no one greater, He swore by Himself, saying, "I WILL SURELY BLESS YOU AND I WILL SURELY MULTIPLY YOU." And so, having patiently waited, he obtained the promise. For men swear by one greater than themselves, and with them an oath given as confirmation is an end of every dispute. In the same way God, desiring even more to show to the heirs of the promise the

unchangeableness of His purpose, interposed with an oath, so that by two unchangeable things in which it is impossible for God to lie, we who have taken refuge would have strong encouragement to take hold of the hope set before us. *This hope we have as an anchor of the soul, a hope both sure and steadfast.*

Hebrews 6:11–19, emphasis mine

It is incongruent for us to have hope in the core of our being and then to become hopeless in a particular area. When this happens, it is evidence we have believed a lie of some kind. For, as the writer of Hebrews points out, our hope is founded upon the Word of God, who cannot lie. When we abandon hope, we are actually expressing *unbelief* in God.

Walking in victory and resisting hopelessness are matters of *faith*, just as avoiding busyness and overcoming fear are matters of faith. Faith is the foundation that sustains dreams in our lives. In the light of faith, we see the falseness of both lack and brokenness as excuses to stop dreaming. Consider a few of the names mentioned above in the "Hall of Faith" in Hebrews 11—the ones we are exhorted to imitate. Abraham was "as good as dead" when he believed God and had a son in his old age (verse 12). His wife, Sarah, also had to believe to "[receive the] ability to conceive" for their dream to be fulfilled (verse 11). I challenge anyone to come up with a situation as "lacking" as this couple's. As for anyone who thinks they are "too broken," we've already examined the life of Joseph. Many of us give away our dreams to far lesser attacks and wounds than he experienced. These men and women all used faith to sustain their hope through every obstacle, and so must we.

If hope is the anchor of our souls, then giving up hope is a sign this anchor has not been established deeply enough to secure our trust—or to get us "in the wheelbarrow" with God.

Hopelessness is a sign we must go back to the foundational realities we have embraced, particularly the foundation of the cross. The message of the cross is that there is nothing so lacking or so broken that God cannot restore and redeem it. When we declare ourselves too broken or lacking to do anything, we are actually denying the cross's power.

No Christian intentionally denies the cross. What usually happens is what the author of Hebrews warns us about: We become "sluggish." Extreme circumstances are not the only tests of our faith; we must also negotiate the gravitational pull of time and the mundane. It is easy to get tired, bored and frustrated. It's easy to take stock of a particular stretch of time and conclude we're not getting any nearer to where we want to be. In this temporal, earthly perspective we appear insignificant and powerless. And if we start to believe it is true, we end up suspecting we don't deserve our dreams anyway. We feel wounded, "heart sick" from "hope deferred" (Proverbs 13:12), and abandon our dreams. The message of the cross is the antidote for sluggishness. The cross not only addresses our wounds of hopelessness; it reveals God's ultimate goal of making us part of a new race, a race destined to bear the perfect image of His Son and to rule and reign with Him in eternity. In light of the cross, our most lofty and audacious dreams pale in comparison to what God intends for us to do and become.

Connecting with our purpose in God charges every part of our lives with hope and passion. You see, in adopting us as His sons and daughters, God has taken an interest in the entirety of who we are, even in our "little" dreams. Indeed, one of His greatest strategies and pleasures is taking things the world regards as insignificant and making them the means by which He displays His glory, power and beauty. (The cross is the supreme example of this revelation; see 1 Corinthians

1:27–29.) Simply put, God takes the seemingly small, insignificant raw material of our lives and fashions us into His masterpieces.

God likes to use the "small" things that we freely give to Him in faith. Consider how impressed Jesus was by an "insignificant" gift:

> He looked up and saw the rich putting their gifts into the treasury. And He saw a poor widow putting in two small copper coins. And He said, "Truly I say to you, this poor widow put in more than all of them; for they all out of their surplus put into the offering; but she out of her poverty put in all that she had to live on."
>
> Luke 21:1–4

No one else would have considered that this widow's gift was greater than those of the rich. But her giving was an act of faith, and in heaven's economy, the smallest act of faith gives God more to work with than all the religious power in the world. It is a glorious thing to learn the secret joy of giving all that we are, including our dreams, to God, whether in seasons of lack, prosperity, joy or pain. Our expression of trust creates the opportunity for God to do something great in our lives.

Around Bethel Church, we use a couple of "one-liners" to express a certain attitude about God. First, we say, "One and God are always a majority." Remembering that "God is with us" must train us to view our circumstances from a position of victory. Success is guaranteed as we continue to become like Christ. Second, we say, "If it matters to you, it matters to God." In fact, if it matters to us, it matters *even more* to God. Never diminish your dreams; instead, make sure you present them as gifts to your Father. He cannot wait to show you what they're all about and to partner with you in a powerful journey toward their fulfillment.

Looking Forward, Looking Back

Matthew Kelly has written a wonderful book titled *The Dream Manager* about a business consultant who stumbled upon the importance of the dreams of a company's employees. In the book, Kelly describes a challenge to list 100 dreams you have and bravely to write them in a journal dedicated to the cause of your dreams. I decided to try it one evening. I wrote for over an hour and counted up the fruit of my bounteous imagination: only 33 dreams! An audible groan slipped through my lips as I settled back to the task. Two hours later, I had my 100. Instead of feeling satisfied by my accomplishment, however, my hope slipped. As I considered the dreams I had written down, I felt that the gap between those dreams and my present reality was too wide to bridge.

Despondent, I closed the journal and went to bed pouting. Lying there, I remembered an experience I'd had several years before in the prayer chapel. While praying for my two sons, I had felt overwhelmed. Frankly, it was a pathetic whining episode before God. Despite that posture, God was merciful and gave me a panoramic vision of myself as an old-time farmer with my hands on a wooden plow. I pushed while two oxen pulled, and we bucked and crawled across a vast land. As I looked past the oxen, I realized the impossibility of the task. Overwhelmed by the sight before me, my heart slid into a puddle of hopeless self-pity. Standing alone in the chapel, feeling completely overwhelmed, I heard God's gentle voice say, "Turn around." Literally turning, I saw that the vision continued behind me, where there were acres and acres of well-plowed fields. I had been working so hard for so long, with such intensity, I had forgotten to look behind me and recognize what I had been accomplishing. God showed me that I had done much, and done it well, in His strength. My furrows were straight and were planted and bearing fruit. I openly wept at God's mercy to show me what was happening in the spirit realm.

Turning back around, I looked to a far mark on a distant mountain. Beginning to plow again, I was renewed. Having grown up on a farm, I had learned that straight furrows are made by keeping your eyes focused on a faraway target. This target is our dream, the far-off place where God wants us to go, and we must stay fixed on it if we are to reach it. However, we can only sustain our focus on the dream by regularly taking time to reflect on what is behind us and around us. Just as Sabbath rest renews our minds and bodies and keeps us from toil, so reflecting on the testimonies of what God has done in our lives renews our ability to see and walk toward our dream.

Dreaming is a process of both looking forward and looking back, of imagining and remembering. It is also a process that takes *time*, as I discovered in listing my 100 dreams. But unless we invest the time to allow our imagination to picture our dreams, we will never reach them.

A friend once told me, "The first rule of success is imagination. If you can't see it, you can't have it." After hearing him say that several times, I cornered him and asked what the second rule was. He said, "My father told me to first dream it. Then, after you have seen it far in the future, let the *long arm of reality* reach out and pull it back into today. Figure out what to do today to bring about that dream."

One of the first ways I took his wise advice was by returning to my dream journal. I turned to the back of the journal and began to list, in reverse order, every success I could recall since my earliest memory. By doing this, I was "closing the gap" between my list of dreams and my current place. I was using the testimony God had given me to encourage myself, remembering all the land I had tilled. Success in the task at hand is directly related to how well and how consistently we are able to connect it with a flow of confidence (gained through our past success) and hope (gained through our vision). Dreaming is a key to creating this flow.

In a private place, linger before the Lover of your soul until you sense God's presence. Ask Him for the grace to dream again. Place your hand on your heart and prophesy to yourself the following prayer:

> Jesus, I am Your beloved and You are mine. I am being perfected by You, the Author and Finisher of faith. You have great plans for me, beyond what I can ask or think, and I cooperate with You. So, I REOPEN my dreams and visions. I RELIGHT my hope. I RELEASE my redeemed imagination. I am a prosperous soul.

6

Bound in Spirit

*And now, behold, bound in spirit, I am
on my way to Jerusalem, not knowing what will happen to me there.*

Acts 20:22

*Courage is the first of human qualities because
it is the quality which guarantees all others.*

Winston Churchill

We often call people of courage "heroes." Cultures throughout
the generations have sought heroes to answer the human hunger
for meaning, and our generation is no exception. We feel our
need for heroes as much in their absence as in their presence.
When a society finds it difficult to identify individuals who give
us glimpses of the nobility of which humanity is capable, it begins to starve for lack of meaning. And hopelessness, cynicism
and lawlessness creep into society and eventually take hold.

Paul identified the source of these hunger pains when he
said:

> For the earnest expectation of the creation eagerly waits
> for the revealing of the sons of God. For the creation was
> subjected to futility, not willingly, but because of Him who
> subjected it in hope; because the creation itself also will be
> delivered from the bondage of corruption into the glorious
> liberty of the children of God.
>
> Romans 8:19–21, NKJV

Futility means "without purpose." Paul is saying that the
purpose of everything in creation hangs upon our purpose,
which is to become sons and daughters of God who rise as
Christlike heroes on the earth. As I explained in Chapter 2,
Jesus is the Desire of all Nations, though the nations do not
yet recognize Him as the Hero for whom they hunger. We are
called to introduce others to their divine purpose by walking
in our own—call it evangelism. Until we "arise and shine,"
not only we, but also the whole world, will suffer for lack of
value and meaning.

In light of this high and holy calling, the aspects of training
in Christlikeness we have explored thus far—wrestling with
our God-given identities, breaking free from lies, taking risks to
restore dreaming, learning to carry abundance—take on their
true heroic dimensions. And as genuinely heroic tasks, they
require courage. We must always associate the virtue of courage
with a prosperous soul. Yes, a prosperous soul is a contented
soul, one who knows how to enjoy good things, who can take
rest and be at leisure, who can dream. Yet the prosperous soul
doesn't stay seated! Remember what my wise friend said about
what comes after dreams: The "long arm of reality" has to
reach for those dreams with wisdom, strength and determina-
tion. In short, a prosperous soul is courageous.

Where does courage spring from? Where do heroes get the
power to make them larger than their fears? Consider this
heroic statement from the apostle Paul:

Now I go bound in the spirit to Jerusalem, not knowing the things that will happen to me there, except that the Holy Spirit testifies in every city, saying that chains and tribulations await me. But none of these things move me; nor do I count my life dear to myself, so that I may finish my race with joy, and the ministry which I received from the Lord Jesus, to testify to the gospel of the grace of God.

Acts 20:22–24, NKJV

If the Holy Spirit warned you or me of "chains and tribulations" lying ahead, wouldn't we likely take such warnings as signs to stay away from those dangers? Paul boldly states that the knowledge he will suffer does not "move" him. The only thing that does move him is the goal of finishing his race with joy. This is his purpose, and to this purpose he is "bound in the spirit."

Here we find the key to courage. A hero's courage is always the result of *a spirit bound to a cause greater than oneself.* The word translated "bound" in the passage above is *deo*, which *Strong's Concordance* tells us is also translated as "bind," "imprisoned," "chained" or "tied." I hope these words have a familiar ring to them. In the preceding chapters we've explored the "bent" that a Poverty spirit creates in our lives, and the word *bent* derives from the same word meaning "to put in bonds." I've also used the term *bondage* to describe the effects of the Poverty spirit. But what we see in Paul's testimony is that not all bonds or bents are negative. In fact, fulfilling our purpose as heroes depends on our being bound to and by certain things.

Freedom

It is understandable that words such as *imprisoned* and *chained* carry strong connotations of oppression, control and injustice. That has been accurate in nearly all cases where those words apply. This association between constraint and oppression gives rise to a similar association with their opposites— words such as *freedom* and *justice* are often defined as a lack of constraint or limitation. We even see this association in Scripture. In the Romans 8 passage above, we are given the promise that creation will be delivered from bondage into liberty. However, there is a point where getting rid of limits fails to create freedom. This truth plays out daily in a society where the deepest and most long-standing bonds that have held us together—including the bonds of marriage and those between parents and children—have become optional in the name of "freedom." This has resulted in tremendous damage to our most basic social units.

This extreme rejection of limits perverts and denies the true nature of freedom recognized by every wisdom tradition in history—including the ones (primarily Greek, Roman and Christian) that informed the framers of our national documents when they plotted our course as a free nation. For thousands of years, wise people have understood that freedom is not created by lack of constraints, but by the right kinds and degrees of constraints. This truth is related to the one we saw in the previous chapter, that people "unrestrained" by vision will perish. Those with vision are restrained by it, and such restraints do not harm life but preserve and promote it.

This wisdom pervades the writings of the apostle Paul. No one in the New Testament, besides Christ Himself, speaks so often and passionately about freedom. Paul's letter to the Galatian church is one of the fiercest defenses of freedom ever recorded. And yet, no other person in the New Testament refers to himself more often as a person in bonds—not merely in physical bonds, but "bound" in his heart to a Person. In fact, other than "apostle," the term that Paul uses most often to describe himself is "servant." The Greek word translated "servant" is the word *doulos*, and its root is *deo*. When Paul calls himself "a servant of Jesus Christ," he is literally calling himself a "bound man."

This paradox of bondage and freedom posed by Paul's life reveals two fundamental truths about the nature of freedom. First, true freedom is not determined by the presence or lack of physical restraints, but by the state of our spirit. Second, this spiritual freedom is not determined by the presence or lack of spiritual bonds, but by *that to which our spirit is bound*.

Before we consider the nature of this spiritual bond, let's take another look at the nature of freedom. Think of someone you know whom you would describe as a free person. What attitudes and behaviors reveal that person's freedom? Is his or her freedom primarily a matter of circumstances or of character?

The *Oxford American Dictionary* defines *free* as "not under the control or in the power of another; able to act or be done as one wishes." According to this definition, Paul reveals himself to be free by stating that nothing is able to "move him" from his chosen course. Of course, Jesus Christ is the prime example of a wholly free person, a man whose self-control was so developed that no one, whether priest, Pilate or the devil himself, could force Him to do anything or divert Him from fulfilling His mission. Jesus proclaimed His freedom with statements such as, "I lay down My life so that I may take it again. No one has taken it away from Me, but I lay it down on My own initiative. I have authority to lay it down, and I have authority to take it up again" (John 10:17–18).

Freedom is not merely the absence of external control, but the presence of self-control. It is the power and skill to direct yourself in a certain way. Without self-control, you cannot be truly free.

Consider the common experience of men and women released from prison. Imagine you have been behind bars for twenty years. You've occupied a constantly monitored six-by eight-foot cell, received standardized food, clothing and health care. You've interacted with a small group of people. You've negotiated an extremely limited range of choices. Then the day comes when your sentence is up. You step out from the prison gates with a few dollars and a bus ticket. Welcome to freedom! It feels so great you could fly. The air is clean and the sky is deep blue. Trees and space are part of your life again, as are privacy and independence.

But that initial rush wears off as you face the reality of life "outside." Suddenly, you are bombarded with choices, choices you aren't sure you're able or ready to handle. Not only have you grown accustomed to having options taken from you, you remember what you did the last time you had options. And if you mess up again, you know well what the consequences will be. The pressure you feel to make the right choices and your fear of making the wrong ones grow into a crushing burden.

Under this pressure, many people reach a point where prison doesn't look as bad as it used to. At least in prison, the rules are clear, one's basic needs are met and safe choices will be made for everyone. This lack of self-control creates a kind of soul-sickness that makes a person vulnerable to the bracing air of the real world. And as long as this sickness remains, the external, artificial life-support system of prison seems preferable.

People who lack the power of self-control cannot be free, so they always end up being controlled by external influences. Solomon expressed this truth in Proverbs 25: "Like a city that is broken into and without walls is a man who has no control over his spirit" (verse 28). While convicted criminals are extreme cases, the truth is everyone lacks the capacity to handle free will perfectly. Thus, we all end up, knowingly or unknowingly, surrendering control in some measure. There are many kinds of prisons that people live in, or go back to repeatedly, some of them seemingly comfortable. For example, women stay in abusive relationships, men struggle with addictions, families labor under massive bondage as debtors and generations settle for welfare cycles that destroy their ambition and vision. Many desire to break free of their circumstances. But once again, our circumstances do not cause the fault lines in our character; they merely expose them. Whether or not circumstances change, those fault lines will continue to cause damage as long as they remain. The question of freedom always boils down to whether we have access to a power that can change us from the inside out, power that can heal our soul-sickness. Until we find that power we will stay in bondage.

Spirit to Spirit

The message of the Gospel is precisely that the power to change us from within exists and has been freely given to us. Our role is simply to appropriate that power through faith. We are taught that when we put our trust in Christ, we receive a new spirit, a spirit animated by and united to His Spirit. And Scripture tells us very clearly He is the source of true freedom and self-control (emphases mine):

> Now the Lord is the Spirit, and where the Spirit of the Lord is, there is *liberty*.
>
> 2 Corinthians 3:17

> The fruit of the Spirit is . . . *self-control*.
>
> Galatians 5:22–23

119

God gave us a spirit not of fear but of power and love and *self-control.*

2 Timothy 1:7, ESV

Notice the term Paul uses to describe self-control: "fruit." In biological terms, fruit is what a plant produces containing the seed of reproduction. We describe the results of human reproduction as the "fruit of the womb." In the realm of the Spirit, spiritual fruit both reproduces the likeness of God in us and enables us to reproduce spiritual sons and daughters as we fulfill Christ's commission to make disciples (see Matthew 28:19). Just as human reproduction involves the most intimate communion between two people, so, too, does spiritual reproduction. The fruit of the Holy Spirit grows in our lives as we commune with Him, spirit to Spirit. This *bond* is the source of our freedom.

The establishment of this spirit-to-Spirit bond between us and the Godhead is the culminating request of Jesus' prayer in John 17:

I do not ask on behalf of these alone, but for those also who believe in Me through their word; that they may all be one; even as You, Father, are in Me and I in You, that they also may be in Us, so that the world may believe that You sent Me. The glory which You have given Me I have given to them, that they may be one, just as We are one; I in them and You in Me, that they may be perfected in unity, so that the world may know that You sent Me, and loved them, even as You have loved Me.

verses 20–23

In essence, Jesus prayed we would have the same relationship with the Father that He has! Think about it: Only the same kind of relationship can reproduce the same kind of fruit. And the reason Jesus came was to reproduce sons and daughters like Himself.

If we observe Christ's life in order to understand the nature of this spiritual bond, we find the same paradoxical counterpoint between bondage and freedom as seen in the life of Paul. Paul used the same word, *doulos*, when he explained that Christ "emptied Himself, taking the form of a *bond-servant*" (Philippians 2:7, emphasis mine). The Son of God became a "bound man." He said, "I do not seek My own will, but the will of Him who sent Me" (John 5:30). He was "led by the Spirit" (Luke 4:1, NKJV). Jesus fully submitted His will to God.

Yet, unlike the scenarios of bondage and submission to which we are accustomed in the world, the bondage and submission of Christ did not rob Him of His freedom. He wasn't turned into a mere puppet. Quite the opposite is true: Never was anyone more free, more master of His will. Surrendering our will to God does not kill it; it requires us to exercise our will every day and every moment in a specific direction. It means choosing to be led by the Spirit. This is the only way to become a hero, a son of God: "For all who are being led by the Spirit of God, these are sons of God" (Romans 8:14).

Observing the submission of Christ and its fruit in His life, we see not merely His peerless self-control but also His wild, radical love, His outrageous joy, His fiery boldness, His deep wisdom and perfect humility. This picture reveals that submission to God is something completely different from what many of us associate with the term. The exuberant, abundant life Jesus lived reminds us we were designed to submit to God, to do what He is doing and say what He is saying. We were designed for intimacy and partnership with Him. When we choose that—building on the grain of divine purpose in us—then fulfillment, success and abundant life are the inevitable results.

Many people mistakenly think that submitting to God— that saying, "Not my will, but Yours"—means losing not only your freedom but also your identity and personality. On the contrary, when you say to Father God, "I want what You want," here's what happens: He smiles and says, "Excellent! I want you to be the person I made you to be. I know you've received a lot of misinformation about that through your experiences so far. But if you'll get in the wheelbarrow with Me, I'll show you who you truly are!" True submission boils down to giving up our distorted, limited versions of reality so we can receive and live in His version. And because His version is the real one, it's the only one in which we can be fully real, fully ourselves.

Friends Live on the Fourth Floor

Jesus told His disciples, "No longer do I call you slaves, for the slave does not know what his master is doing; but I have called you friends, for all things that I have heard from My Father I have made known to you" (John 15:15). This is a definitive statement for us to understand why being bound to God's agenda is so liberating and fulfilling. Our relationship with God as His supernatural stewards is not a typical boss–employee relationship. Yes, we serve Him, but as mature sons and partners in the family business. We are bound in spirit because His interests are our interests. And as mature sons, partners and friends, we enjoy full disclosure about what our Father is up to (see John 15:15). This knowledge is to shape our perspective in everything.

Over time I have identified four levels of perspective on our lives. And I have observed that people are living on one of these four levels at any given time. I call these levels of perspective *Tactics*, *Strategy*, *Vision* and *Purpose*. I like to picture these as four floors in a building, each providing a different kind of knowledge that supports our perspective on life.

Tactics is the ground floor where we see *what* we are doing. Here we daily negotiate the details of our practical choices. It's easy for us to spend a lot of our time looking at life from this perspective, because these details demand constant attention. Some people even make their careers on this level—they receive formal training to become "knowledge workers," experts at administrating endless facts and decisions. Many perfectionist types thrive on the tactical level, because they can narrow their focus to things they have the power to change or control. It is easy, on this level, to glamorize toil. Limiting yourself to managing practical choices without giving attention to larger questions can lead you to become a highly skilled expert who appears successful on the outside but is an emotional disaster on the inside. You were made to live on a higher level.

Strategy is the floor where we see *how* we are doing things. We see how the details of our choices and experiences fit together, and thus are able to make plans and set goals. Occupations that require abstract thinking and decisiveness, such as counseling, teaching and various leadership roles, attract people who live on this level. Career strategists are usually highly driven people who can work through complex or extended assignments, always managing to display a sense of direction and priority. However, the limitations of this perspective will cause them to struggle with control, insecurity and intolerance of others.

Vision represents the third floor, allowing us to see *where* we are going in life. Living on this level is much more fulfilling, for it meets our need to have a "big picture" for our lives. However, if we mistake this for the highest level of perspective, we risk living from a picture that may seem noble, inspiring and good, but that actually falls short of why we ought to be going there. Settling on this level sets us up to mistake our dreams and plans for our purpose, and thus to struggle when we experience disappointment. How many people do you know who work hard serving a vision their entire adult lives, only to wake up one day and wonder, *How did I get here? Does any of this even matter?* Most midlife crises are the fruit of living on the third floor. Vision must come under the revelation of our divine Purpose.

Purpose is the final floor, the level where we see *why*—why we are here, why we are doing what we're doing and why we're going where we're going. Purpose is what we must bind our spirits to. Only when we are bound to divine purpose will we correctly marshal the information from the three lower floors. We see this throughout the Bible. Many of the heroes of faith used tactics, strategies and vision in ways that are completely counterintuitive to the natural mind. Before the disciples grasped Jesus' purpose, they were usually confounded by the way He thought and did things. To Peter, it was insane for Jesus to say in one moment He was the Messiah and speak in the next of being taken and killed. Jesus, whose purpose was to go to the cross, rebuked him: "Get behind Me, Satan! You are an offense to Me, for you are not mindful of the things of God, but the things of men" (Matthew 16:23, NKJV). Living from any level other than divine purpose makes room for a perspective that resists God. We are designed to be supernatural stewards. And possessing full disclosure of what God is up to makes us responsible to align each level of perspective under Purpose. Over the years, I've counseled hundreds of people in various states of crisis who ask, "What should I do about this?" Their problems range from career choices to professional and personal challenges, financial threats, business start-ups and terminations. In every case, I show them how to work from the top floor down in order to align their perspective. I begin by asking the person to identify their Purpose (the top floor). Once Purpose is identified, they write out their Vision (what they see from the third floor), followed by Strategies (the long arm of reality of the second floor), and finally a list of Tactics (the details of living on the ground floor). Time after time, this simple tool has enabled believers to identify sound choices that have integrity with who God made them and has called them to be.

I encourage you to run your own challenging questions through this tool. Think of your most pressing problems and identify which floor they hail from. Most often the problems of life appear as tactical issues. Write them down and set them aside. Then focus on answering this question: Why am I here?

Stewards of His Presence

I developed this "Four Levels" tool after discovering my own need for higher perspective in deciding whether to invest in a business. Calculations reign supreme for CPAs, so I first approached the decision by cranking out data *ad nauseum*. After fretting and worrying over the numbers, I realized they wouldn't reveal anything unless I had defined an investment strategy against which to test them. So I set to work defining my life's investment strategy. After a while, I saw that a strategy to make wealth would only materialize when I could define my vision (what I could see) for my wealth.

Defining my vision pushed me beyond the range of financial tools and into the realm of study and prayer. As I was praying one day in the Alabaster House, I had a vision, like a snapshot in my mind's eye. I saw a black room illuminated by a single spotlight, which was focused downward on the center of the floor. In the pool of light sat a large canvas bag with a dollar sign printed on the side. It was tied at the top, slumping loosely and clearly filled with something valuable. As I snapped out of the vision, I excitedly asked God what it all meant. He answered, "This is the wealth of the nations."

My first thought was that God was about to share the secret of the transfer of wealth from the world to the Church, a promise I've long sought to see fulfilled. I began to pace the room in excitement, praying for provision and breakthrough in finances and waiting for God to show me more. Then the picture snapped open again before my mind's eye. I saw the same dark room and the bag in the spotlight, only this time the bag was untied and lying on its side. Gold coins of many nations and small bars of brilliant yellow spilled onto the floor. I asked God what this development meant, and immediately He answered, "This *is* the transfer of wealth from the wicked to the righteous." Nearly jumping from my skin, I thanked God and asked Him what I should do. He said, "Teach My stewards."

God was putting His finger on the purpose for which He had designed me. Teaching was in me like grain in wood. From that point, my responsibility was to align my vision, strategies and tactics with this purpose.

It was clear to me that the vision of the moneybag linked our supernatural stewardship with managing the wealth of the nations. Thus, one of my top priorities in teaching stewardship was to discover and impart keys for handling abundance. When Jesus said, "He who is faithful in a very little thing is faithful also in much" (Luke 16:10), He revealed that faithfulness is the quality required to handle abundance.

Yet faithfulness is not determined by whether or not we have abundance. What is the true source of faithfulness?

Paul declared:

> It is a trustworthy statement: For if we died with Him, we will also live with Him; if we endure, we will also reign with Him; if we deny Him, He also will deny us; *if we are faithless, He remains faithful*, for He cannot deny Himself.
>
> 2 Timothy 2:11–13

Like self-control and freedom, faithfulness comes from God Himself. Only He can teach us what it means to be faithful to Him and to our purpose. Just as He reproduces His other divine attributes in us, He reproduces His faithfulness through spirit-to-Spirit communion.

For this reason, building and deepening our devotional life with God is at the center of our calling as supernatural stewards. Above stewarding money, talent, time or any other resource, our top priority must be learning to steward the source of all of them: His presence. This is our first purpose, for only in the place of worship, prayer and meditation—the place of friendship—will our Father disclose to us the unique design and purpose He has placed in us. Until we establish that top floor in our thinking, we will inevitably mishandle our stewardship.

Finally, stewarding the wealth of nations will challenge the Church to succeed where we (and the world) have so often failed. I believe God is calling an entire generation of Josephs to rise to this challenge. And that call is necessarily to become stewards of His presence, for only those who know how to "practice His presence"—to carry the awareness of that spirit-to-Spirit bond wherever they go—will be able to access the courage they need to face that challenge.

When God presented Joshua with the revelation of his purpose to lead the Israelites into the Promised Land, He said,

"Have I not commanded you? Be strong and courageous! Do not tremble or be dismayed, for the LORD your God is with you wherever you go" (Joshua 1:9). His presence with us is the source of our courage. And only those who are bound in spirit with Him will steward their connection with His presence above all. Only they will follow Him in facing the challenges that require great courage. Only those who are bound in spirit will not "be moved" by anything but Him.

Take some time alone with God and ask yourself what you are bound to. Often, the answer lies behind us. The decisions and behaviors that follow us are a grand display. Look into your checkbook and observe where you spend your money. This, too, will give clues to what you find most important. Write everything down that you identify and present it all to your Father in heaven as an offering. Take your time, and listen to what He has to say.

7

Spirit of Mammon

No one can serve two masters; for either
he will hate the one and love the other, or
he will be devoted to one and despise the
other. You cannot serve God and wealth.

Matthew 6:24

In *Mere Christianity*, C. S. Lewis points out:

[The devil] always sends errors into the world in pairs—pairs
of opposites. And he always encourages us to spend a lot of
time thinking which is the worse. You see why, of course?
He relies on your extra dislike of the one error to draw you
gradually into the opposite one. But do not let us be fooled.
We have to keep our eyes on the goal and go straight through
between both errors. We have no other concern than that
with either of them.[1]

In the voyage of the prosperous soul, the supernatural
steward must navigate between two primary hazards: Pov-

erty and Mammon. To draw on C. S. Lewis's analogy above, these two are one of the devil's pairs of opposite errors; they are designed to bend us off course in one direction or the other. So far we have studied lack and how it robs us of power, dreams and passions. We have seen how we must allow God to restore our souls so we may fulfill our call as stewards. But as our dreams and passions awaken, and the Lord entrusts us with more, we must learn to guard against the hazard of Mammon. You see, Mammon also wants us to have passion, power and dreams. But it does not want us bound in spirit to steward these things for divine purpose. It has another purpose for them, a purpose that comes directly from hell.

The word *mammon* (Greek, *mammonas*) has fallen out of use these days, and modern Bible translators have rendered it in several ways. The New American Standard Bible uses "wealth," while others like the New International Version prefer "money." Each of these is an unfortunate attempt to capture a word unfamiliar to our Western minds. *Mammonas* is something different from riches, money or wealth. It means to personify wealth by placing our trust in it, to deify it as a god. It means to worship it.

We often relegate the term *worship* to what we do in a Sunday morning service. So let me refresh your thinking about what it means to treat something as a god. *Worship* comes from an Old English word that means to acknowledge the worth of something. In its most basic meaning, worship has to do with how we perceive and attribute value to things. A person worships whatever he or she determines to have the highest value. In turn, whatever has the highest value in our life will define our value for everything else. Worship is therefore unavoidable. Even the agnostic and atheist renders worship to his or her own supreme value.

From Genesis to Revelation, the Bible shows that acknowledging God's worth as the highest will enable us to value everything else properly. When we value other things above God, however, we'll treat things and people in the wrong way. Our country's Declaration of Independence is built on this principle. It states, "We hold these truths to be self-evident, that all men are created equal, that they are endowed by their Creator with certain unalienable Rights, that among these are Life, Liberty and the pursuit of Happiness." Our forefathers recognized that justice—treating people as they ought to be treated—can only be pursued on one foundation: the recognition of our equal value as endowed by our Creator. Every struggle for justice in our nation, from the Civil War to women's suffrage and the civil rights movement, has been fought on this foundation.

Injustice persists in our nation and around the globe, however, because humans cannot ultimately sustain justice unless they worship the Creator who gives them value. If we say human worth derives from our Creator, then we are saying (1) His worth is greater than ours, and (2) we can only properly recognize our value by properly recognizing His. Jesus emphasized this when He said to the Pharisees:

> Woe to you, blind guides, who say, "Whoever swears by the temple, it is nothing; but whoever swears by the gold of the temple, he is obliged to perform it." Fools and blind! For which is greater, the gold or the temple that sanctifies the gold? And, "Whoever swears by the altar, it is nothing; but whoever swears by the gift that is on it, he is obliged to perform it." Fools and blind! For which is greater, the gift or the altar that sanctifies the gift?
>
> Matthew 23:16–19, NKJV

As Jesus says, the gold in the temple and the gift on the altar receive their value and purpose from something greater than themselves. Likewise, we receive our value and purpose from the One who created us. Yet, like the Pharisees, we'll remain foolish and blind to our own value and purpose unless we establish God as our supreme value. Worshipers understand that everything—including the goods, services and resources we assign value to in the marketplace—must first be seen and understood from a heavenly value system. Without drawing value and purpose from our Source, we will inevitably mishandle our lives and resources.

The Bent of Mammon

Mammon leads us to treat money as the most valuable thing. When we allow material wealth to define our value system, it creates a bent in us that is just as destructive as the Poverty spirit. Like the Poverty spirit, the spirit of Mammon is not something we can simply cast out of a person. It gains a place of influence in us by growing strong first in our ears and eyes, and then in our trust—our heart. Ultimately it is worshiped in its victims' lives. It can only be displaced as we listen to and trust in the truth.

I remind you of the central message of prosperity: In the Kingdom, there is always enough because God is without limit and Christ has declared us worthy to receive all that is His as His sons and daughters. It is this precious relationship with Him that determines our worth and what we deserve. Unlike the message of Poverty, which denies our worth, the message of Mammon pretends to agree with it. It says, "There's always enough for me, because I deserve it." It claims to deserve things on the basis of self, apart from relationship with God. Thus, where Poverty is self-defeating, Mammon is self-aggrandizing. Where Poverty shames, Mammon flatters. Where Poverty starves our ability to love or hope, Mammon inflames our lust and greed. Where Poverty steals power from us, Mammon thrusts power upon us.

The emotional, financial and spiritual masquerade offered by Mammon appeals to our natural appetites. For this reason, it is easily misinterpreted as God's favor finally apprehended. It is possible to pray long for the breakthrough, only to find we fumble the ball in the moment we receive it by falling prey to Mammon and making agreement to serve material wealth in order to serve ourselves.

Mammon produces the following fruit in our lives: First, Mammon urges us to use the power of wealth to acquire things and to attract people to ourselves. It manipulates our need for acceptance and significance by promising us that wealth can buy us meaningful connections and a compelling image. It also manipulates our natural attraction to beautiful things and people by inflaming our desire to possess them.

Second, Mammon works to destroy loyalties and relationships because it demands allegiance to money and self above others. This allegiance, left unchecked, will blossom into extortion, deception and all manner of shady dealing. This in turn breeds suspicion, competition and division, including faction-building, an us-versus-them mentality and comparison of ourselves to others. These are all fingerprints of the Mammon spirit.

Third, Mammon encourages sensual living, creating a sense of entitlement to a steady flow of comforts, pleasures and signs of wealth in our life. This sense of entitlement eventually becomes an oppressive demand that works to betray us into slavery, both to debt and to addiction. Addictions such as pornography, gambling, overeating and all manner of excess (living beyond our means) are symptomatic of the spirit of Mammon. Indeed, I suspect most addictions are rooted in the Mammon spirit.

The sins of Mammon begin subtly enough, but they end more spectacularly than the sins of Poverty because they are empowered by wealth. Greater power always yields greater results. And power makes a way for what is in our hearts to come out. Many Christians fear money because of the blatant damage done by those who possess wealth. They misinterpret money as "the root of all evil,"[2] when Jesus says it is the *love* of money that is at evil's root. They point to lottery winners, overnight pop stars, bankers, politicians and businessmen who have been seduced by Mammon and conclude that an abundance of money is hopelessly deceitful. The problem with this categorical conclusion is that fear of money's seduction is itself a seduction. Fear of money is actually part of Poverty; through this fear our enemy traps us, as Lewis described, in an opposite error.

We can see the enemy's fingerprints in both errors by what they have in common, namely, the true root of all evil: pride. While Poverty promotes a negative focus on self and Mammon promotes a positive focus, they both lead us to focus on ourselves above God or others. As a result, both spirits work to cut us off from all that God has for us.

First, they cut us off from the work of the cross. Poverty denies the cross by crushing us with condemnation and shame, convincing us we're too broken to change. Mammon denies the cross by stuffing us with things, drowning out our hunger for forgiveness and restoration.

Second, they both cut us off from our adoption as a son or daughter, and with that from our identity. Poverty keeps us a "nobody" and Mammon keeps us endlessly trying to become "somebody" through accumulation and achievement.

Finally, they both cut us off from our purpose and legacy as prosperous souls and supernatural stewards. In drawing attention to ourselves, Poverty and Mammon keep us from looking up and looking out. That is, they keep us from seeing what is greater than ourselves, which is the necessary ingredient for us to rise to our potential greatness. And they keep us from embracing a lifelong vision, the "race" of which Paul spoke. A self-focus always leads us to seek instant gratification over pursuing a higher cause.

Paul described the destructive effects of a Mammon agenda and its utter incompatibility with God's agenda:

> It is obvious what kind of life develops out of trying to get your own way all the time: repetitive, loveless, cheap sex; a stinking accumulation of mental and emotional garbage; frenzied and joyless grabs for happiness; trinket gods; magic-show religion; paranoid loneliness; cutthroat competition; all-consuming-yet-never-satisfied wants; a brutal temper; an impotence to love or be loved; divided homes and divided lives; small-minded and lopsided pursuits; the vicious habit of depersonalizing everyone into a rival; uncontrolled and uncontrollable addictions; ugly parodies of community. I could go on.
>
> This isn't the first time I have warned you, you know. If you use your freedom this way, you will not inherit God's kingdom.
>
> Galatians 5:19–21, The Message

The End of the Affair

What happens when Mammon infects a culture—when it becomes nationalized? Here's what happens: Our right to the pursuit of happiness becomes synonymous with the compulsion to pursue wealth. Allowing wealth to determine our system of values inevitably leads to corporate mishandling of resources and people. Our nation's culture is unmistakably bent by the worship of wealth. Virtually all the symbols of

135

success and happiness have to do with garnering more and protecting what we have. In turn, all the fruit of this value system infects our cultural influencers of religion, economy, government, family, arts and media, science and education.

Many people want to blame the abuses of our consumer culture on capitalism, but that indictment is shortsighted. Personal property, free enterprise and private profits are powerful tools in the creation, growth and sustainability of the greatest nations on earth. The problem is that these have been wrongly used to advance our worship of wealth. What is missing in capitalism is the worship of God on a national scale. Hearts are not changed by handing over control of resources to the state, as any version of totalitarianism from the last century attests. The experiments in communism, fascism and Nazism revealed that changing the system leads only to poverty, despair and devastation. In fact, recent history reveals that the devil has blinded people to the real source of sin located in their hearts. As a result, whole countries have been tricked into swinging away from one error and into the other.

The pursuit of wealth has been a core value in our nation from its inception. However, this pursuit used to be governed under our faith in God, expressed as a vision for freedom, justice and community. Now it seems that being the wealthiest nation takes priority over being the freest or most just.

The widespread influence of Mammon will be displaced only when we repent of our money-driven value system and establish God as our supreme value. Jesus was clear that only one thing could occupy that place of value in our hearts:

No one can serve two masters; for either he will hate the one and love the other, or he will be devoted to one and despise the other. You cannot serve God and [Mammon].

Matthew 6:24

Our love affair with money must come to an end. This is why I am both concerned and encouraged by current events, as dismal as they seem. As I said in chapter 2, seasons of shaking are always important opportunities to awaken us, test our priorities and call us to fresh engagement with our purpose to be salt and light in the world. This is true for believers and unbelievers alike. The world recognizes this, coining phrases such as "meaning want" and "post-materialist values." In his book, *A Whole New Mind*, Daniel Pink asserts we are replete with abundance and information. He states, "We live in an era of abundance, with standards of living unmatched in the history of the world. Freed from the struggle for survival, we have the luxury of devoting more of our lives to the search for meaning."[3] He has touched on where the developed world finds itself. We have come upon a historic window of opportunity where we are looking for meaning beyond that offered by Mammon.

As always, Jesus Christ holds the answer. We must recognize that the restoration of our freedom and strength does not lie in eschewing wealth, but in learning to love God above all else. This is what Jesus tried to teach the rich young man in Matthew 19. His instruction for the man to sell his possessions was a condemnation not of his wealth but of his love affair with wealth. Jesus was not exposing that sin for judgment's sake but in order to invite him upward to something infinitely better. The blindness caused by Mammon was exposed in the ruler when Jesus laid a far superior offer on the table—"Come, follow Me" (verse 21)—and the young man couldn't see it.

After this encounter, Jesus explained to His disciples how hard it is for the rich to enter the Kingdom. But he reminded them, "With people this is impossible, but with God all things are possible" (verse 26). God wants to do the impossible in

America through His people. First, He wants to free us forever from Mammon by unveiling Himself as the love our hearts truly long for. The Lover of our souls wants to romance us, to take us on an adventure that will put to shame every thrill and pleasure Mammon offers. He wants to meet our needs for significance, power, beauty, relationships and happiness. He wants to satisfy our souls as only He can, for He designed our desires to be satisfied by Himself. Then He wants us to become a revelation of His love to the world, exposing their false love of wealth and giving them a taste of "true riches."

Making Friends

When we allow God to lead us on the adventure for which He made us—when we jump into the wheelbarrow He's pushing—He will set us straight about what money is for. Scripture tells us Mammon has put our relationship with money backward. It is not money that gives us power, but God that gives us power to make wealth:

> But you shall remember the LORD your God, for it is He who is giving you power to make wealth, that He may confirm His covenant which He swore to your fathers, as it is this day.
>
> Deuteronomy 8:18

Recognizing wealth as an assignment reinforces the covenant between us and God. This perspective reveals the true purpose of money: to empower the agenda of our partnership with God. This is the lesson of the parable of the unjust steward:

> Now He was also saying to the disciples, "There was a rich man who had a manager, and this manager was reported to him as squandering his possessions. And he called him and said to

him, 'What is this I hear about you? Give an accounting of your management, for you can no longer be manager.' The manager said to himself, 'What shall I do, since my master is taking the management away from me? I am not strong enough to dig; I am ashamed to beg. I know what I shall do, so that when I am removed from the management people will welcome me into their homes.' And he summoned each one of his master's debtors, and he began saying to the first, 'How much do you owe my master?' And he said, 'A hundred measures of oil.' And he said to him, 'Take your bill, and sit down quickly and write fifty.' Then he said to another, 'And how much do you owe?' And he said, 'A hundred measures of wheat.' He said to him, 'Take your bill, and write eighty.' And his master praised the unrighteous manager because he had acted shrewdly; for the sons of this age are more shrewd in relation to their own kind than the sons of light. And I say to you, *make friends for yourselves by means of the wealth of unrighteousness, so that when it fails, they will receive you into the eternal dwellings.*"

Luke 16:1–9, emphasis mine

The right stewardship of money serves to build relationships. The unjust steward made friends out of his master's debtors by extending grace to them and canceling portions of their debt. Likewise, we are to use our resources to extend grace to unbelievers and invite them to experience the cancellation of debt in Christ. We are to show them what it's like to be a friend of God.

When God is our supreme value, we will use money in service to His priorities, defined by His value system. And heaven's value system is forever defined by the cross. In sacrificing His Son, God sent the human race a message: "I value you as much as I value Myself." As mind-boggling as it is, God has given us the highest place of value in His heart, and He showed His value of us by giving. "For God so loved the world, that He gave . . ." (John 3:16).

The prosperous soul loves to emulate the radically gener-ous God who has "freely [given] us all things" (Romans 8:32). Indeed, the prosperous soul loves to give as a friend gives. A friend does not merely give when you are in need. A friend gives to honor and show affection. This is a "fourth floor" perspective, built on eternal purpose. It orients us to invest our resources in the only things that are going to last forever—God and people. Because of this, we understand that the most valuable resources are not those that can feed and clothe the body, but those that can save, heal, deliver and restore the whole man. These are the "true riches" of the Kingdom.

Jesus says, "If you have not been faithful in the use of un-righteous wealth [mammon], who will entrust the true riches to you?" (Luke 16:11). Embedded here is Christ's promise that our faithful use of money will signal to the world we are to be trusted with the grace and power of heaven. Bill Johnson points out that millions of dollars in a person's bank account cannot provide the miracle that so many of us need for our health, relationships and souls, but that riches in our heavenly bank account can. The more we experience the true riches for ourselves, the more absurd it looks to put money at the top of our value system. Instead, our hunger will grow for the substance of Kingdom realities.

I believe God is calling an entire generation of believers to steward the wealth of the nations. And our capacity to carry wealth depends on a true understanding of its value and purpose, which only comes when our hearts have attached themselves to their true treasure:

> But store up for yourselves treasures in heaven, where neither moth nor rust destroys, and where thieves do not break in or steal; for where your treasure is, there your heart will be also.
>
> Matthew 6:20–21

When our hearts are in heaven creating a storehouse of true riches, we will harness wealth for heavenly purposes. Again consider Joseph. His ability to harness the wealth of Egypt for divine purpose did not come from any human strategy, but from a storehouse of supernatural gifting in divine revelation that he had been developing throughout his thirteen years in captivity.

The Mind of a Steward

Our thinking as prosperous souls and supernatural stewards must begin with the truth that *all things are ours*. We already have full access to our heavenly inheritance of true riches. We don't have to wonder if God wants to equip us with supernatural power to do the works of Jesus. We must simply get in the wheelbarrow with Him and ask Him to show us how to use what He has given us. For only what we learn to use will truly become our own. Jesus stated:

> And if you have not been faithful in the *use* of that which is another's, who will give you that which is your own?
>
> Luke 16:12, emphasis mine

God wants us to experience the benefits of all He has promised us as coheirs with Christ. He wants us to possess the territory He has given to us. But possession only comes through use, and proper use only comes through a value system built on a heart that acknowledges Him as our supreme value.

Our thinking must also be built on the truth that power to make wealth comes from God alone. The Bible is filled with warnings about the wicked who misuse the power endowed by the Creator for their own ends. It reminds us that even though the wicked seem to be prospering, we can be sure that things will not end well for them. We must not be deceived by the appearance of false prosperity around us, but continue to trust in the Source of our power and our resources. Finally, our thinking must be built on the truth that the purpose of all creation is to serve our divine purpose as sons and daughters of God (see Romans 8:19–21). When we are bound in spirit to this purpose, we receive keys of authority to unlock the storehouses of resources that have been designated to help us fulfill our purpose.

Breaking Free of Mammon

Recognizing Mammon in our lives can be approached in two ways. Both involve asking the Holy Spirit to search us and reveal the truth about our values. First, we can examine the fruit of our lives. The presence of addiction, comparison to others or efforts to impress people are signs our values are askew. Second, we can focus on identifying what holds supreme value in our hearts. What is the treasure your heart feeds on and communes with? Agree with whatever the Holy Spirit reveals to you, receive His forgiveness and repent of your trust in Mammon by asking Him to establish the message of Kingdom prosperity in your thinking. Ask Him to awaken your heart and establish Himself as your first and greatest love.

Next, ask the Lord to establish His value for people in your heart. If He is your supreme value, then like Him you will treat others as more valuable than yourself. Paul taught, "Do nothing from selfishness or empty conceit, but with humility of mind regard one another as more important than yourselves" (Philippians 2:3), and, "Be devoted to one another in brotherly love; give preference to one another in honor" (Romans 12:10).

Ask also for the grace of giving and prepare to be radically generous. Macedonia was a territory that had suffered generations of warfare and economic hardship. But in the midst of such lack, God granted the Macedonian church a supernatural grace of giving:

> Now, brethren, we wish to make known to you the grace of God which has been given in the churches of Macedonia, that in a great ordeal of affliction their abundance of joy and their deep poverty overflowed in the wealth of their liberality. For I testify that according to their ability, and beyond their ability, they gave of their own accord, begging us with much urging for the favor of participation in the support of the saints, and this, not as we had expected, but they first gave themselves to the Lord and to us by the will of God. So we urged Titus that as he had previously made a beginning, so he would also complete in you this gracious work as well.
>
> 2 Corinthians 8:1–6

Note the progression here. The Macedonians gave themselves first to God, then to the church. This heavenly system of values positioned them to receive the grace to surpass natural limitations and supernaturally steward their resources according to divine purpose: "participation in the support of the saints."

Paul used the testimony of the Macedonians to teach and encourage the Corinthian church. This tells us that our own breakthrough in the grace of giving will help to release other believers into their divine purpose:

> So I thought it necessary to urge the brethren that they would go on ahead to you and arrange beforehand your previously promised bountiful gift, so that the same would be ready as a bountiful gift and not affected by covetousness. Now this I say, he who sows sparingly will also reap sparingly, and he who sows bountifully will also reap bountifully. Each one must do just as he has purposed in his heart, not grudgingly or under compulsion, for God loves a cheerful giver. And God is able to make all grace abound to you, so that always having all suf-

ficiency in everything; you may have an abundance for every good deed; as it is written, "HE SCATTERED ABROAD, HE GAVE TO THE POOR, HIS RIGHTEOUSNESS ENDURES FOREVER." Now He who supplies seed to the sower and bread for food will supply and multiply your seed for sowing and increase the harvest of your righteousness; you will be enriched in everything for all liberality, which through us is producing thanksgiving to God. For the ministry of this service is not only fully supplying the needs of the saints, but is also overflowing through many thanksgivings to God.

2 Corinthians 9:5–12

Next, become a Joseph who will release other Josephs into supernatural stewardship. How is this done? By waging the warfare of generosity to destroy a Mammon spirit. This is where giving begins. Give yourself and your finances first to God and then to the saints, and give beyond your ability as you crush the enemy of Mammon under your heel. Don't borrow to give (another trap of Mammon), but give sacrificially. Allow yourself to feel inconvenience for the sake of someone else.

Building a new habit in your life usually requires a concentrated period of doing that new activity consistently and intentionally. Because you are called to generosity as a lifestyle, you will probably need to practice giving in a specific way for a specific measure of time. In that way, you can break out of old Mammon-inspired patterns and into the grace of giving. Ask the Lord to show you what such a season of giving will look like in your life. Ask Him to show you how to use His money to make friends for eternity. And then give with joy:

God loves (He takes pleasure in, prizes above other things, and is unwilling to abandon or to do without) a cheerful (joyous, "prompt to do it") giver [whose heart is in his giving].

2 Corinthians 9:7, AMP

8

Dominion

And the Lord said, "Who then is that faithful
and wise steward, whom his lord shall make
ruler over his household, to give them their
portion of meat in due season? Blessed is that
servant, whom his lord when he cometh shall
find so doing. Of a truth I say unto you, that
he will make him ruler over all that he hath."

Luke 12:42–44, KJV

Can you imagine being commissioned to wield the authority of the most powerful man in the world? It happened to
Joseph. How hard is it for you or me to imagine it happening to us?

I once had a unique opportunity to imagine the life of
the powerful while on a family trip to Brunswick, Georgia.
A friend took us to visit a historic private club on St. Si-
mon's Island, where many families of wealth and influence
recreate. Walking through high-ceilinged rooms filled with

antique furniture and original paintings, I was impressed by the grace of "old money." The wall of one hallway was covered with photographs of famous people—I recognized Queen Elizabeth, Franklin Roosevelt, Jimmy Carter and many other statesmen, entertainers and business leaders of the 1930s through the 1980s.

At one point our friend whispered, "Over here. Come inside." We exited the hallway, closing a tall oak door behind us. As our eyes adjusted, we saw a simple square room with more pictures on the walls, dominated by a large circular table at the center. The table was made of massive pieces of beautiful wood and appeared to be custom built for the room. Around the table sat eight chairs, each marked with a brass plate for whose place it represented: *The Honorable George W. Bush, United States of America. The Honorable Tony Blair, United Kingdom.* The others had names of leaders from France, Japan, Italy, Germany, Canada and Russia. This was the very table used in the 2004 G8 Summit, where the most powerful figures in the world had presided over the world's problems and challenges.

I sat in every chair, feeling a little foolish at first, but soon was amazed by the tangible power still resident in that room years later. I sensed, in some small measure, the weight that rests upon statesmen, and I thought again of Joseph and Pharaoh. This time, I found myself even more impressed by the actions of Pharaoh. Joseph said that God made him "a father to Pharaoh and lord of all his household and ruler over all the land of Egypt" (Genesis 45:8). Pharaoh not only authorized Joseph but came under Joseph's divine authority. What king submits to a thirty-year-old man he has just met and authorizes him to govern a nation with the full measure of his powers? Only one who is able to recognize that such a man knows what it means to walk in dominion.

This is the destiny of the supernatural steward: to father the leaders of nations and to influence regions with the Gospel. Few of us may be positioned, as Joseph was, at a political summit. Regardless of our appointments, however, each of us can influence the world from endless placements within our culture. Our calling is not dependent upon how close to the top we find ourselves. Jesus described us as salt and yeast, and the nature of these elements is that they are mixed into things. We are called to father the nations from any part of culture in which we find ourselves. But the nations will submit to our influence, as Pharaoh did, only when we learn to walk in dominion.

I am well aware that dominion—like prosperity, miracles and many other powerful biblical concepts I've been using in this book—is fraught with negative associations. Various movements have abused the concept of dominion, for example by seeking things as ends in themselves rather than as "signs following" those who seek first the Kingdom. The gifts must not be confused with their Giver. However, neither must the gifts and promises of God be suppressed or ignored in reaction to human mistreatment of them. In faith, we must press forward to take hold of God's promises, resisting everything that would disqualify us from receiving all that He has for us.

Believers certainly cannot afford to mistreat or ignore the issue of dominion, which runs throughout the Bible from beginning to end. The Bible begins with God designing and commissioning humanity to take dominion of the earth (see Genesis 1:26–28). It ends with the promise that we will "reign forever and ever" (Revelation 22:5). Yet, lest we think dominion is merely a past and a future reality, Paul reminds us, "Those who receive the abundance of grace and of the gift of righteousness will *reign in life* through the One, Jesus

Christ" (Romans 5:17, emphasis mine). Dominion is to be our present reality.

Joseph walked in dominion because he was trained as a steward. Other than Christ, no one in Scripture more clearly models "training for reigning." The qualities we develop through stewardship are the same qualities that enable us to reign in life. And that training is largely focused on establishing divinely ordered relationships—first between us and God, and then between us and all else. We've seen how these relationships are intimately connected by examining the damage that occurs when they are out of order. But what does it look like when they are in order? What happens when we have fully submitted our trust to God and are bound in spirit to His purposes? What happens when our partnership with Him in fulfilling these purposes directs our use of the things He has entrusted to us? The answer is we have dominion. Dominion is the reality we were designed to live in as mature sons and daughters of God.

Dominion, by definition, brings together two dimensions: authority and ownership. So to understand dominion, we have to understand how these two elements function together.

Authority

A fundamental principle of authority is that it can only be given to you, and when it is given, it is always related to a specific set of tasks. In civil society, when a person uses a position of authority to do things he or she has not been authorized to do, we call it abuse. Likewise, when a person fails to fulfill the duties he or she has been authorized to fulfill, we call it negligence. Both scenarios are grounds for removing a person from their position of authority. This is why it is important for us not to talk vaguely about the "authority of the believer" without being very clear about just what it is we have been authorized to do.

The Greek word translated "authority," *exousia*, is also translated "power" or "right." Consider what the apostle John said about the *exousia* of the believer:

> But as many as received Him, to them He gave the right (*exousia*) to become children of God, even to those who believe in His name.
>
> John 1:12

Walking as children of God is the defining, fundamental task we have been divinely authorized to perform. This means it is not simply a good idea to leave behind Poverty in order to imitate Christ; it is imperative.

As mature sons, we are authorized to teach others:

> All authority has been given to Me in heaven and on earth. Go therefore and make disciples of all the nations, baptizing them in the name of the Father and the Son and the Holy Spirit, teaching them to observe all that I commanded you; and lo, I am with you always, even to the end of the age.
>
> Matthew 28:18–20

We are in a family business—and our business is making family. Every aspect of fulfilling our purpose works through relationship. The Great Commission did not come with a ten-step model or a business plan. It came with Christ's promise to be with us always, showing us how to be sons like Him and how to invite others into sonship. Our authority to walk in dominion comes from God as we follow His lead in everything.

Jesus' masterful self-control in submitting to His Father's will was the key to His freedom. It was also the key to His authority. To exercise His authority as the Son of God to destroy every work of the devil, Jesus had always to stay under authority, doing and saying only what the Father was saying and doing. We must increasingly establish the same unwavering commitment: to have no other agenda than to be "about [our] Father's business" (Luke 2:49, NKJV) as Christ did from His earliest years. Then we will be able to exercise the authority He has given us.

Signs of Authority

This issue of Jesus' authority always surrounded His ministry. It began with His temptation in the wilderness, when the devil tried to tempt the Lord to misuse His authority as God's Son. It continued with religious leaders demanding to see Christ's credentials for teaching and performing miracles. It ended only in Jesus' last moments of life, when mockers yelled for Him to prove Himself by coming down from the cross. For those people in His life who had eyes to see and ears to hear, however, such as Nicodemus and the centurion in Luke 7, the issue was perfectly clear: Jesus wouldn't have been able to perform all His divine acts unless He was under divine authority.

> Rabbi, we know that You have come from God as a teacher; for no one can do these signs that You do unless God is with him.
>
> John 3:2

> But just say the word, and my servant will be healed. For I also am a man placed under authority, with soldiers under me; and I say to this one, "Go!" and he goes, and to another, "Come!" and he comes, and to my slave, "Do this!" and he does it.
>
> Luke 7:7–8

Jesus didn't need to use sales pitches or pages of arguments and proofs; His supernatural actions spoke for themselves. These are the actions that stewards in dominion offer to people. And our management of the family business is meant to produce the same supernatural results Christ produced. Jesus Himself insisted that the supernatural results of His ministry were the evidence of His divine authorization. And He gave His audience the right to dismiss Him if they didn't see those results:

> The works which the Father has given Me to accomplish—the very works that I do—testify about Me, that the Father has sent Me. . . . If I do not do the works of My Father, do not believe Me; but if I do them, though you do not believe Me, believe the works, so that you may know and understand that the Father is in Me, and I in the Father.
>
> John 5:36; 10:37–38

Yet Jesus also made clear His miracles were not random manipulations of the natural world; they were in fact encounters with His Father's Kingdom. His supernatural results were the result of heaven coming to earth.

Jesus was able to bring heaven to earth for two reasons. First, heaven was the reality He lived in (see John 3:13, NKJV). And second, the Father had authorized Him to release this reality on earth. When Jesus healed diseases, multiplied food, cast out demons and raised the dead, He was giving people a taste of what God's family members can expect of a Kingdom without disease, poverty, torment, fear or death. Thus, His every encounter while on earth served the Father's business of drawing people into His family and establishing His Kingdom "on earth as it is in heaven."

The only way to make disciples is the way Christ made them. If we are to undertake His commission to make disciples, we must learn to live in heaven's reality as He did and release it to those around us. This conviction drives one of the central messages we preach at Bethel Church: The Body of Christ owes people encounters with the Kingdom of heaven. I'm not speaking of some religious obligation to evangelize. I'm referring to a divine mandate inherent in the work of the cross. At the cross, Christ paid a price for every human being to be restored as a son or daughter in His Kingdom. But though He paid that price for us all, He cannot get what He paid for without our trust. This is Christ in you, the hope of glory (see Colossians 1:27). The more we trust Him, the more we experience the benefits of the heavenly inheritance He bought for us: healing, deliverance, deepening intimacy with the Father, joy, peace, revelation, hope and all the "true riches" of heaven.

At Bethel we have seen God release to us astounding supernatural wealth: miracles of physical and emotional healing, financial provision, relational restoration, as well as revelation, dreams and visions. We have been overwhelmed by the same realization that the lepers had in the days of Elisha:

> For the Lord had caused the army of the Arameans to hear a sound of chariots and a sound of horses, even the sound of a great army. . . . Therefore they arose and fled in the twilight, and left their tents and their horses and their donkeys, even the camp just as it was, and fled for their life. When these lepers came to the outskirts of the camp, they entered one tent and ate and drank, and carried from there silver and gold and clothes, and went and hid them; and they returned and entered another tent and carried from there also, and went and hid them. Then they said to one another, *"We are not doing right. This day is a day of good news, but we are keeping silent; if we wait until morning light, punishment will overtake us. Now therefore come, let us go and tell the king's household."*
>
> 2 Kings 7:6–9, emphasis mine

When you realize Christ has paid the price for everyone to taste and experience the same goodness that you have, it becomes hard not to tell—and show—the rest of the world what they're missing. You become possessed with a sense of justice for Christ. His sacrifice deserves nothing less than all humankind. The Moravian missionaries expressed this in their motto: "To win for the Lamb that was slain the reward of His sufferings."[1] This is the passion that drives the supernatural steward to mature from one who has received true riches to one who distributes them.

Ownership

When we're spiritually immature, we primarily receive. When we reach maturity and dominion, we act as generous benefactors distributing the supernatural abundance of our Father's Kingdom. This pivotal change or revelation that takes place in us is that of taking ownership. Jesus told us, "[Our] Father has chosen gladly to give [us] the kingdom" (Luke 12:32). This promise seems vague and overwhelming until we see we can't fully manage the family business without having access to its resources. It would be inconceivable for God to authorize Jesus to fulfill His destiny as the Messiah without also giving Him the wealth of the Kingdom to back that authority. Likewise, Joseph could hardly oversee his storehouse strategy in Egypt without being able to act as owner of the nation's resources. All authority must be provided with a measure of ownership. And dominion, by definition, requires the ownership of a kingdom.

When we have a revelation of ownership, we use what we have been given. Consider this description of Solomon's dominion:

> Solomon's *provision* for one day was thirty kors of fine flour and sixty kors of meal, ten fat oxen, twenty pasture-fed oxen,

153

a hundred sheep besides deer, gazelles, roebucks, and fattened fowl. *For he had dominion* over everything west of the River, from Tiphsah even to Gaza, over all the kings west of the River; and he had peace on all sides around about him.

1 Kings 4:22–24, emphasis mine

Solomon's dominion was seen in his ability to harness the wealth of the land for kingly purposes. So it is with mature believers who walk in dominion. Paul's ability to access Christ's strength in every kind of situation, Joseph's ability to access divine revelation every time he was presented with a dream, Jesus' ability to heal all who came to Him—all are defining marks of mature sons of God who know how to use their spiritual possessions.

The ease with which Jesus dispensed miracles or Joseph interpreted dreams seems a long way from our experience. Expecting the goodness of God to always show up is difficult to imagine when the thought of car repairs or bounced checks makes our blood pressure rise. This is when we must engage our faith, believing that God will not stop taking us "line upon line, precept on precept" until we know (1) what we possess in the Kingdom, (2) the purpose for those possessions and (3) how to use them in the service of God's purposes. Simply put, we must believe that God will give us revelation.

You cannot use money sitting in your bank account that you don't know about. And you cannot use your heavenly inheritance without revelation. In fact, revelation is one of the resources we are to steward. Paul said of his fellow apostles, the mature teachers, "Let a man regard us in this manner, as servants of Christ and stewards of the mysteries of God" (1 Corinthians 4:1). The mysteries of God are the deep, spiritual realities He reveals to those who trust Him. We must "digest" these realities until they become our reality.

The writer of Hebrews explains that "digesting" revelation requires us to exercise our senses in a specific way:

> For though by this time you ought to be teachers, you have need again for someone to teach you the elementary principles of the oracles of God, and you have come to need milk and not solid food. For everyone who partakes only of milk is not accustomed to the word of righteousness, for he is an infant. But solid food is for the mature, who because of practice have their senses trained to discern good and evil.
>
> Hebrews 5:12–14

When we practice tuning out the message of Poverty or Mammon and tuning in to the message of prosperity, we are exercising our senses to discern good and evil. We are training our minds to interpret that data according to truth. It's called "exercise" because it requires our active participation. When God instructed me to declare, "I am significant," He was giving me "solid food"—revelation of my real, heavenly identity. Just trying to digest this revelation exposed how far my self-perception was bent away from the truth. But as I exercised my senses with this truth, it grew to become my reality. My senses were able to discern the evil designed to undermine my significance as well as the good designed to affirm it. And because I used the truth, it became my possession. This means I now can give it away to others. When I tell someone, "You are significant," I say it with the authority of my personal experience and training. I am not merely quoting a biblical truth; I am releasing revelation as a mature teacher.

This is how we learn to walk in dominion as stewards. We release the heavenly reality we have learned to live in through faithful use of the revelation God communicates to us. This is why our prayer life with God is so important. The "true riches" God gives us can only come through relationship.

Spiritual maturity comes to us as we learn to live in His presence and join Him in what He is doing and saying.

Living in the River

Scripture is clear that dominion is first an inner reality. Unless we have rule over our spirit and possess our soul, we will not be able to rule and possess much of anything. This is why I have spent so much time in the preceding chapters focusing on the realm of the soul. The servant whose soul, or senses, are trained to discern good and evil is one whose mind, will and emotions express the thoughts, desires and impulses of a son of God. We possess our souls in the same way we train our senses, as Jesus instructed:

> But before all these things, they will lay their hands on you and persecute you, delivering you up to the synagogues and prisons. You will be brought before kings and rulers for My name's sake. But it will turn out for you as an occasion for testimony. Therefore settle it in your hearts not to meditate beforehand on what you will answer; for I will give you a mouth and wisdom which all your adversaries will not be able to contradict or resist. You will be betrayed even by parents and brothers, relatives and friends; and they will put some of you to death. And you will be hated by all for My name's sake. But not a hair of your head shall be lost. By your patience possess your souls.
>
> Luke 21:12–19, NKJV

Jesus taught us to possess our souls by learning to patiently depend on the presence of God in every circumstance. As we see in this passage, He wants us to know about the storms we will face as His stewards, but He doesn't want us to worry about them. He wants our souls to be trained to ignore all fear and to receive the purposes and resources of heaven. He wants our minds to be "set . . . on the things above, not on the things that are on earth" (Colossians 3:2). Thus, though we are not to "meditate beforehand" about various challenges that await us, we are to meditate on the heavenly reality.

I want to share a meditative exercise I discovered when I interacted imaginatively with a picture of heaven found in Revelation. (Exercising our imaginations is a dimension of exercising our senses.) This exercise has had a profound effect in training me to prosper my soul, exercise my senses and increasingly recognize what it means to walk in dominion. I invite you to enter into this exercise by first allowing the richness of John's vision to fill your mind's eye:

> Then he showed me a river of the water of life, clear as crystal, coming from the throne of God and of the Lamb, in the middle of its street. On either side of the river was the tree of life, bearing twelve kinds of fruit, yielding its fruit every month; and the leaves of the tree were for the healing of the nations. There will no longer be any curse; and the throne of God and of the Lamb will be in it, and His bond-servants will serve Him; they will see His face, and His name will be on their foreheads. And there will no longer be any night; and they will not have need of the light of a lamp nor the light of the sun, because the Lord God will illumine them; and they will reign forever and ever.
>
> Revelation 22:1–5

The river of God is the quintessential image of abundant life, supernatural provision and prosperity. Everything good you will ever need or desire can be found in it. It runs through the middle of the street, giving everyone full access to it. All you need to do is learn how to get in its flow.

Now, engage your imagination further by activating your body. Stand up and imagine you are standing in the river, facing downstream, away from the Throne. Behind you, God is placing good things into the river for you. Yet, because of your position, you remain a spectator, watching good things float past you, just out of reach. Try to envision what some of those good things might be. Speak this prayer aloud:

> Father God, I am standing in the crystal river of heaven that flows from Your Throne. You fill this river with good things, but because I am facing downstream, good things flow away from me. They are just beyond my reach, too hard to catch.
>
> Lord Jesus, I want to turn. I want to see Your throne. I want to see your provision. I turn around, in Jesus' name. [Physically turn and face the opposite direction.]
>
> Thank You, God, that I am facing upstream. I can envision the throne of God and the Lamb. Good things are coming to me. The good things are everywhere. There's more than I can contain. There is abundance here for everyone. In Jesus' name, Amen.

Imagine what it looks, sounds, smells, tastes and feels like to stand in the flow of this river's immeasurable abundance. There is no limitation, no lack. God places good things in this river for you and everyone connected to you. These good things flow toward you and they're easy to catch. The new position you now occupy creates a new paradigm of expectations. Facing the Source of abundance drives away the fear, insecurity and powerlessness you previously felt as you watched good things pass you by. From this new view, you expect good things. You expect that every need will be met at the right time. You expect that nothing will be impossible. You know that everything in your Father's Kingdom is yours.

In my life, the river has been a tool for training my thinking away from a lack paradigm to a paradigm of plenty. I remember walking away from the river prayer looking for good things to drift into my hands. They did. I began to recognize opportunities and favor that had previously passed me by. I grabbed everything I could get my hands on. An opportunity presented itself, a request to serve someone I admired. I enthusiastically accepted one offer and then another and another. I began to make more and more decisions from faith, with the expectation of good. Soon I was wondering how to handle so much good, as my cup was overflowing. My friends noticed. My wife noticed. I noticed—and I liked it. I had entered the Holy Spirit School of Dominion.

As I learned to manage the things God was entrusting to me, I discovered that maintaining my position in the river wasn't easy. I learned it was natural to face downstream, lowering my expectations and losing my focus on the Throne. By contrast, it is supernatural to believe God, to keep my expectations fixed on the Throne, as the smart farmer keeps his gaze on the high point in the distance. When discouragement, insecurity, fear of failure or fear of missing out alerted me to my "downstream" expectations, I renounced my agreement with the lies of Poverty and turned around to expect the reality of prosperity.

Eventually, as my divine purpose came into clearer focus, I went beyond believing for good things. Now I had begun to believe God would give me the best—everything I needed and more to fulfill all He had put in my heart to do. This expectation added further skills and knowledge to my management. First, I learned that, while everything in the river is good, they are good, better or best for me in relation to my purpose and the season of my life. It meant I had to stop saying yes to every opportunity and learn to say no to some

159

of them. Sometimes I missed opportunities and let God's best pass me by. This proved to be an lesson for me to learn that God is wildly faithful and generous, and that He has many more "bests" for me.

I also learned to pass on to others certain things that came my way. Facing upstream makes us openhanded, comfortable with any level or kind of possessions and able to use those possessions for any purpose for which the Master earmarks them. What is not mine belongs to someone else, and when I partner with God in releasing His provision, then when I need more, mine will be there.

The more I gave, the more I became comfortable with the authority God had entrusted to me. I understood I was blessed to be a blessing, and that I could be trusted to influence people. This gave me confidence and made me even more proactive in becoming one who faithfully distributes rations to God's household (see Luke 12:42–43). I began to act like the head and not the tail (see Deuteronomy 28:13).

I also learned to rest. I realized that my initial racing around in the river, trying to get everything I could, had actually been a sign I did not fully trust in God's inexhaustible supply of good gifts. Thus I had not yet taken dominion as a steward. Gradually I learned to rest in the goodness of God, not trying to get things but simply standing in the flow of the river and receiving them.

I learned something else in the river, something I call "positioning." While we don't need to run around the river grabbing for good things, we do often need to position ourselves in a certain way to receive what God is sending to us. Years ago, God blessed me with the ability to form my own company and prepare tax returns. The extra dollars and friendships that grew from this time were treasures in my heart. Later, I had to downsize and eventually sell the business in order to position myself for new assignments. Such transitions in life can be difficult and scary—like negotiating the slippery rocks and currents while crossing a river. But it is worth it when you get to your appointed place in the river and capture that best thing God has for you. My new "best" was the opportunity to teach and write. It has been one of the greatest challenges of my life to reengineer myself from accountant to author and teacher. But I'm living a dream and feeling God's favor in it. Above all, I love the adventure of learning to respond to Him, following the wind of His Spirit to new places in the river, rejoicing at the surprises and gifts He sends me and delighting in our partnership of generosity to all around me. Nothing is more fulfilling and exhilarating than embracing the call to be His faithful steward.

Conclusion

Pray again now, with a view *upstream*. Close your eyes, if you wish, and say this aloud:

Father God, heaven is flowing toward me. There is no limitation in heaven. God places good things in the river and those good things flow to me. They are easy to catch when I face the throne of God.

I do not need everything I find in the river because God will send me many bests. I will not settle for good or better, only God's best.

I am resting in the river. God, teach me to see and hear. Teach me to feel, taste and smell opportunities. Teach me prosperity and dominion. Amen.

9

The Art of Purpose

When Joseph interpreted, a king changed course. When supernatural stewards distribute the true riches of heaven, the world is "turned upside down" (see Acts 17:6). Or, rather, it is turned right side up, by tasting heaven. The bright-line distinction between the limitations of the natural world and the limitless provision of heaven is the supernatural steward's portion. This distinction inherently attracts attention, as God fully intends it to do. Scripture resounds with promises and prophecies concerning God's long-standing purpose to release such great blessing through His people in ways that draw the attention of nations. He plans to minister an "evangelism of jealousy" through us by displaying that we undeniably have something the world doesn't have and wants. As Paul tells us, it is not judgment and intimidation but His goodness and kindness that draw people to repentance (see Romans 2:4).

The blessings of God certainly include material wealth, but the true riches that will attract nations are much greater. Jacob's blessing from God was not more livestock or gold, but a declaration of identity and purpose that changed him from the inside out and released him into an entirely new life. Supernatural stewards understand that the blessings we want and most need are those that bring divine transformation. They equip us with the capacity to carry and direct all the resources, both natural and supernatural, that God wants to flow through our hands. You see, transformation is what the world truly hungers for. People are all too familiar with the abuse and broken relationships created by the influence of Poverty and Mammon. On some level, they recognize that throwing money at problems, whether personal or social, is not enough. Nothing in the material world can ultimately satisfy, change or heal the brokenness of the human heart or clean up the messes it creates.

The blessing that will make supernatural stewards famous is the same blessing that once drew the Queen of Sheba to leave her kingdom and discover for herself if the outrageous report she had heard was true. This report was not of a man blessed with enormous wealth but with the ability, like Joseph's, to interpret "difficult questions" better than any other wise men and soothsayers of the day. In the end she told Solomon:

> It was a true report which I heard in my own land about your words and your wisdom. Nevertheless I did not believe their reports until I came and my eyes had seen it. And behold, the half of the greatness of your wisdom was not told me. You surpass the report that I heard.
>
> 2 Chronicles 9:5–6

Wisdom is the blessing we must seek as supernatural stewards, as Solomon did. It is the blessing that will release an evangelism of jealousy.

Solomon's famous encounter with God, in which he asked the Lord for wisdom, gives us the keys for seeking this blessing:

In that night God appeared to Solomon and said to him, "Ask what I shall give you."

Solomon said to God, "You have dealt with my father David with great lovingkindness, and have made me king in his place. Now, O Lord God, Your promise to my father David is fulfilled, for You have made me king over a people as numerous as the dust of the earth. Give me now wisdom and knowledge, that I may go out and come in before this people, for who can rule this great people of Yours?"

God said to Solomon, "Because you had this in mind, and did not ask for riches, wealth or honor, or the life of those who hate you, nor have you even asked for long life, but you have asked for yourself wisdom and knowledge that you may rule My people over whom I have made you king, wisdom and knowledge have been granted to you. And I will give you riches and wealth and honor, such as none of the kings who were before you has possessed nor those who will come after you."

2 Chronicles 1:7–12

This encounter is astounding in many ways, but there are three things I want to focus on. First, Solomon did not stumble blindly into this encounter. He understood the truth of the moment in which he was standing. He was standing in the fulfillment of God's promise to David. Solomon recognized and embraced his divine purpose to rule Israel. He had inherited this purpose through his father David's favor with God—and he was bound in spirit to that purpose, having no other agenda. Second, Solomon did not ask for wisdom and knowledge in general. He asked for wisdom and knowledge to rule. He understood that divine wisdom is always attached to divine purpose. And it is always attached to dominion. Third, the implication of God's response to Solomon is that his request for wisdom indicated his fitness to carry everything else.

165

To receive the blessing of wisdom, the Body of Christ must first realize we are standing in the fulfillment of a promise that our Father made to Christ, the son of David. In fact, David prophesied about this promise in one of his Messianic psalms:

> I will surely tell of the decree of the LORD: He said to Me, "You are My Son, today I have begotten You. Ask of Me, and I will surely give the nations as Your inheritance, and the very ends of the earth as Your possession."
>
> Psalm 2:7–8

Our participation in the fulfillment of this promise is two-fold. We are part of the "nations" that the Father is giving to Christ, His "inheritance in the saints" (Ephesians 1:18). But we are also Him—the Body through which He is taking possession and dominion of the ends of the earth. And once again, our call to walk in dominion in Christ is not solely reserved for "the Millennium," but is a call to reign in life now.

The more we recognize and embrace dominion as our divine purpose, the more we will see that our greatest need is for the blessing of wisdom. Solomon did not simply ask for wisdom because his father told him to do so. He deeply understood that it was the key to handling his dominion successfully. Without this blessing, he would have always been limited in his ability to handle any blessing. Likewise, without wisdom and knowledge to rule—that is, to direct our lives and resources according to our divine purpose in God—we will never be fit to carry the "more" that God has for us. Thankfully, the more we see this and seek God for the blessing of wisdom, the more He will give it to us—along with everything else!

Take a moment to think about your prayer life in light of Solomon's request. What things do you find yourself consistently asking of the Lord? Do you primarily ask for His intervention in various circumstances? Or, do you ask Him for the wisdom and strength to expand your capacity and skill to deal with circumstances from a place of greater dominion?

The Stairway

Scripture wonderfully describes the tangible results produced under Solomon's rule by divine wisdom. These results deserve to be treated fully in another book or two. Taken as a whole, however, Solomon's wisdom and knowledge created dramatic results in every area of social, political and religious life in Israel and among the surrounding nations. First Kings 4 describes a number of these results, including:

A large, well-fed, happy population:

Judah and Israel were as numerous as the sand that is on the seashore in abundance; they were eating and drinking and rejoicing.

verse 20

Service and tribute from lesser kings and kingdoms:

Now Solomon ruled over all the kingdoms from the River to the land of the Philistines and to the border of Egypt; they brought tribute and served Solomon all the days of his life.

verse 21

Abundance of food:

Solomon's provision for one day was thirty kors of fine flour and sixty kors of meal, ten fat oxen, twenty pasture-fed oxen, a hundred sheep besides deer, gazelles, roebucks, and fattened fowl.

verses 22–23

167

National peace and safety:

For he had dominion over everything west of the River, from Tiphsah even to Gaza, over all the kings west of the River; and he had peace on all sides around about him. So Judah and Israel lived in safety.

verses 24–25

The eradication of poverty and the establishment of individual property for all the citizenry:

. . . every man under his vine and his fig tree, from Dan even to Beersheba, all the days of Solomon.

verse 25

Human resources, transportation and effective infrastructure:

Solomon had 40,000 stalls of horses for his chariots, and 12,000 horsemen. Those deputies provided for King Solomon and all who came to King Solomon's table, each in his month; they left nothing lacking. They also brought barley and straw for the horses and swift steeds to the place where it should be, each according to his charge.

verses 26–28

An internationally renowned treasury of literature, art, music and knowledge of creation:

He also spoke 3,000 proverbs, and his songs were 1,005. He spoke of trees, from the cedar that is in Lebanon even to the hyssop that grows on the wall; he spoke also of animals and birds and creeping things and fish. Men came from all peoples to hear the wisdom of Solomon, from all the kings of the earth who had heard of his wisdom.

verses 32–34

Above all, the greatest expressions of Solomon's wisdom were his temple and his palace. These "houses" contained the lion's share of his foreign policy work, his administrative skills, his royal wealth and his architectural and artistic talents. They were the visible monuments by which Solomon brought to fulfillment God's promises to David—the promises that David's son would be king and would build the house of God. At the heart of these monuments, shining like a jewel, was the one thing that held them together, the thing that left the Queen of Sheba "breathless":

> When the queen of Sheba had seen the wisdom of Solomon
> . . . and *his stairway by which he went up to the house of the
> Lord, she was breathless.*
>
> 2 Chronicles 9:3–4, emphasis mine

This stairway is a picture of access and intimacy, a physical reality of the relationship designed to exist between the King of kings and His "kings and priests." The stairway was literally the channel of Solomon's divine wisdom. Through it he had something that no other kings of his day had, yet what we believers today have in the Holy Spirit: communication with heaven. Our privilege to inquire of the Lord enables us to give the world what they don't yet have. Thus, stewarding the wealth of Israel in order to build these two awe-inspiring structures and the stairway between them was only one stage of Solomon's divine purpose. His ultimate purpose was to use them. The Lord appeared to Solomon and reminded him of this other, more important stewardship after the consecration of the temple:

> Thus Solomon finished the house of the Lord and the king's
> palace, and successfully completed all that he had planned
> on doing in the house of the Lord and in his palace. Then

the Lord appeared to Solomon at night and said to him, "I have heard your prayer and have chosen this place for Myself as a house of sacrifice. . . . I have chosen and consecrated this house that My name may be there forever, and My eyes and My heart will be there perpetually. As for you, if you *walk before Me* as your father David walked, even to do according to all that I have commanded you, and will keep My statutes and My ordinances, then I will establish your royal throne as I covenanted with your father David, saying, 'You shall not lack a man to be ruler in Israel.'"

2 Chronicles 7:11–12, 16–18, emphasis mine

Tragically, Solomon's success in stewarding the building of these houses was followed by his failure to steward the thing that mattered most to God: the relationship that was to be lived out in them. God's priority is not that we accomplish a certain set of tasks but that we "walk before Him." What we do matters only if it is what He is doing and if we're doing it with Him—that is the only key to success. When this center falls out of our lives, everything falls with it. As soon as Solomon began to abandon the stairway of intimacy, obedience and partnership with God in favor of other intimacies and partnerships, he started a downhill slide toward losing his kingdom. His source of wisdom was cut off.

Solomon knew His relationship with God was the source of his wisdom. Throughout Proverbs, he did not speak of wisdom as some disembodied virtue, but of the Person of Wisdom, who is clearly the Holy Spirit. The implication is that there is no getting wisdom without getting Him. Solomon was under no illusions about the source of his blessing and the secret of his success. So, why did he walk away from Him? It is the same question we ask of Lucifer, who fell from the presence of God in heaven, or of Adam and Eve, who fell from the paradise of Eden. When conditions were perfect, abundant, beautiful and filled with the presence and goodness of God Himself, why have men and angels made choices that cut them off from it all? The answer is that at some point they believed a lie. Their ears and affections turned from the Lord to themselves or others, and their hearts became divided, causing them to buckle under the weight of all they had previously been able to carry.

Scripture tells us that in Solomon's case, man pleasing—which is also the fear of man—was the deception that turned him from the Lord. Solomon's diplomatic alliances with his many wives eventually encroached on his loyalty to God. Ironically, it was Solomon who wrote, "The fear of man brings a snare, but he who trusts in the LORD will be exalted" (Proverbs 29:25). Solomon's tragic ending began quietly as a departure from the clear guidelines for leadership from God in Deuteronomy 17.

When you enter the land which the LORD your God gives you, and you possess it and live in it, and you say, "I will set a king over me like all the nations who are around me," you shall surely set a king over you whom the LORD your God chooses, *one* from among your countrymen you shall set as king over yourselves; you may not put a foreigner over yourselves who is not your countryman. Moreover, he shall not multiply horses for himself, nor shall he cause the people to return to Egypt to multiply horses, since the LORD has said to you, "You shall never again return that way." He shall not multiply wives for himself, or else his heart will turn away; nor shall he greatly increase silver and gold for himself.

Now it shall come about when he sits on the throne of his kingdom, he shall write for himself a copy of this law on a scroll in the presence of the Levitical priests. It shall be with him and he shall read it all the days of his life, that he may learn to fear the LORD his God, by carefully observing all the words of this law and these statutes, that his heart may not be lifted up above his countrymen and that he may not turn aside from the commandment, to the right or the left, so that he and his sons may continue long in his kingdom in the midst of Israel.

verses 14–21

Solomon's testimony is a clear warning about one of the strongest influences we must resist as supernatural stewards who will attract the attention of nations. Knowingly or unknowingly, the people we are called to bless and bring to the Lord will seek to gain the place of priority in our lives. When we truly carry and distribute wealth, both natural and spiritual, one of our biggest challenges will be to make sure our compassion and desire to bless others never usurp the stairway in our lives. As soon as they do, the burden and demand of human need will crush us. We can only maintain a prosperous soul that looks on every need through the lens of prosperity by maintaining the stairway.

Jesus modeled the priority of the stairway for us in His life and ministry. The gospels show us that Jesus was generous beyond measure in meeting the needs of the broken people who came to Him. But they also show us that He walked straight past many needs, because it was not need that moved Him. Only the Father held that place in His heart, as Christ must hold in ours. This is what Jesus referred to when He said:

Do not think that I came to bring peace on the earth; I did not come to bring peace, but a sword. For I came to SET A MAN AGAINST HIS FATHER, AND A DAUGHTER AGAINST HER MOTHER, AND A DAUGHTER-IN-LAW AGAINST HER MOTHER-IN-LAW; and A MAN'S ENEMIES WILL BE THE MEMBERS OF HIS HOUSEHOLD. He who loves father or mother more than Me is not worthy of Me; and he who loves son or daughter more than Me is not worthy of Me. And he who does not take his cross and follow after Me is not worthy of Me.

Matthew 10:34–38

The One who commanded us to love one another only did so after insisting that He alone must be our first love. And that love must be expressed by our obedience to His voice above all others.

As supernatural stewards, we must receive the full benefit of Solomon's powerful testimony of both success and failure. History clearly demonstrates that a society rises or falls according to the choices of those appointed to hold dominion over it. In his success, Solomon led Israel into its golden age; in his failure, he led them into a decline from which they never recovered. When the fate of a nation is at stake, our connection with God's presence is vital. And the fate of nations is precisely what is at stake in our choice to love Him above all else and make His agenda our own in everything.

Wisdom and Knowledge

Let's look a bit more closely at the blessing of wisdom. The account of Solomon's request in 1 Kings adds considerably to the picture in 1 Chronicles above:

> "Now, O LORD my God, You have made Your servant king in place of my father David, yet I am but a little child; I do not know how to go out or come in. Your servant is in the midst of Your people which You have chosen, a great people who are too many to be numbered or counted. So give Your servant *an understanding heart to judge Your people to discern between good and evil.* For who is able to judge this great people of Yours?"

It was pleasing in the sight of the Lord that Solomon had asked this thing. God said to him, "Because you have asked this thing and have not asked for yourself long life, nor have asked riches for yourself, nor have you asked for the life of your enemies, but have asked for yourself discernment to understand justice, behold, I have done according to your words. Behold, I have given you a *wise and discerning heart*, so that there has been no one like you before you, nor shall one like you arise after you."

1 Kings 3:7–12, emphasis mine

As we saw in the previous chapter, discernment of good and evil is something we develop as we learn to perceive and use Kingdom revelation. Wisdom, knowledge and understanding are other dimensions of this ability, which also must be developed through training our senses. Thus, one of the primary things we are asking for when we request the blessing of wisdom is an anointing to learn. We are asking the Holy Spirit to fulfill His assignment from the Father to "guide [us] into all the truth" (John 16:13).

The apostle John said the following about this learning anointing we receive from the Holy Spirit:

As for you, the anointing which you received from Him abides in you, and you have no need for anyone to teach you; but as His anointing teaches you about all things, and is true and is not a lie, and just as it has taught you, you abide in Him.

1 John 2:27

Now, John was one of the original people commissioned by Jesus to teach and make disciples. Therefore, it may seem strange for him to tell us we don't need teachers. But John understood that his role as a teacher was all about showing people how to learn from the Holy Spirit. Only the Holy

Spirit can impart to us His anointing for learning, without which we cannot perceive revelation. No person was ever meant to, or ever could, fulfill the role of the Holy Spirit in our lives. We are to sit under His anointed teachers, yet we are to discern their anointing by observing if their teaching increases our confidence in and need for the Holy Spirit rather than for the teacher.

Likewise, the Bible was never designed to fulfill the Holy Spirit's role. We use the metaphor of a *sword* for the Bible because we recognize it as a tool that will not use itself. It must be wielded by a skillful swordsman, and there is none better than the One who forged it for His own use in our lives. If we let Him, He will use Scripture as a tool to lead us into all truth—and I think "into" is a very telling preposition. One of the primary things the Bible reveals is that truth cannot be reduced to mere ideas. Truth is correspondence to reality. The Holy Spirit leads us into all truth by training us in every dimension of our being to live in heavenly reality.

We know the Holy Spirit is leading us into all truth when in reading the Bible we find its apparent contradictions and mysteries begin to resolve into a coherent pattern that, though it remains beyond our power to fully comprehend, makes very deep and thorough sense to us. It stirs us to think with the logic of heaven, which is often paradoxical—its truth found in the tension between opposing truths.

We see, for example, the pattern of Kingdom logic in the gospel accounts of Jesus' miraculous multiplication of food. On both occasions, Jesus instructed His disciples to collect the leftovers after everyone had eaten their fill and then to count the baskets. This instruction shows us the nature of Kingdom generosity. On the one hand, God is a God of abundance, which means He always pours out more than enough to meet our needs. On the other hand, He is not wasteful.

The food in the baskets had a value and a purpose, and was to be stewarded as much as the food that was eaten. In the Kingdom, we are to be both liberal and conservative with our resources.

Scripture is filled with testimonies and principles that can point us down the "ancient paths" of wisdom by which we can increasingly live in Kingdom reality. The true challenge is to faithfully trust the Holy Spirit's lead as He uses Scripture to bring us up against aspects of heavenly reality. These realities may at first appear strange, illogical, convicting or even offensive. Our natural instinct is to shy away from the things that make us uncomfortable. But so often, discomfort is one of the greatest signs we are being positioned to learn something new.

Christians would do themselves a big favor by expecting that being led "into all truth" will at times be uncomfortable, overwhelming or even scary. But we must also expect that it will always be good. That's how it is with God. His reality is very different from our reality. Heaven's patterns and principles surpass the patterns and principles of the natural world. The natural world experiences cycles of increase and loss, but the Kingdom of God is always increasing (see Isaiah 9:7). While natural crops generally produce once a year, the trees of life in heaven produce fruit every month (see Revelation 22:2). As for gravity and the other laws of physics, Jesus regularly exposed them as flexible under the influence of heaven. We can be sure His disciples were often uncomfortable with these encounters. But they pushed through that discomfort and became men and women who turned the world upside down by releasing similar heavenly encounters. If our lives are going to correspond to heavenly reality, then they will necessarily express a different pattern, with different results, from those of most people around us.

How do we come to understand what it means to conform to the pattern of heaven? We do it by obeying God's instructions, by discovering that the One pushing the wheelbarrow is trustworthy and by experiencing how wonderful it is to take that thrilling journey. Only those who obey God can tell you it works.

Take tithing as an example. It is usually one of the first indicators to new Christians that God's people relate to money differently in His Kingdom from how we did in the world. People who have grown up in church but live under the influence of Poverty may struggle to understand why they are to give to God of their limited resources when He clearly has no need of them. But anyone who sets his or her heart to honor God by practicing tithing will soon discover what it actually is: an ancient path of wisdom that godly men and women have walked since the beginning of time (from Abel to Abraham through to the present day). It is a practical demonstration of the truth that God rightfully deserves our first and our best in everything and that giving this to Him will position us to receive His blessing. Paul states in his letter to the Romans, "If the firstfruit is holy, the lump is also holy" (Romans 11:16, NKJV). Setting apart the firstfruit for God effectively sets our entire lives apart to Him.

The Lord told Israel that withholding their tithes from Him was robbing Him of what was rightfully His. As a result, the "devourer" was robbing them of what was theirs. God was so passionate about getting His people out from under the curse of this thievery that He laid out a challenge and, essentially, a bribe to rouse their curiosity about the tithe:

> "Bring the whole tithe into the storehouse, so that there may be food in My house, and test Me now in this," says the LORD of hosts, "if I will not open for you the windows of heaven and pour out for you a blessing until it overflows. Then I

will rebuke the devourer for you, so that it will not destroy the fruits of the ground; nor will your vine in the field cast its grapes," says the LORD of hosts. "All the nations will call you blessed, for you shall be a delightful land," says the LORD of hosts.

Malachi 3:10–12

Tithing is one of the practices that lead us into this divine exchange of the Kingdom. The final result of applying the wisdom of the tithe—of bringing our lives into alignment with the law of firstfruits—is that the nations will acknowledge the blessing of God on us.

Life as Art

There are many other keys of wisdom the Holy Spirit wishes to unlock for us in order to bring our lives and resources into congruity with heavenly reality. Related to the tithe is the wisdom of the storehouse. Scripture refers to three different storehouses: our personal storehouse (savings), the storehouse in God's house (the Church) and the storehouse of heaven. These are the repositories of heaven's banking system, which brokers both natural and supernatural resources as we participate in God's pattern of giving and receiving. I believe we are to direct our resources into all three storehouses and learn the ways in which they are related.

Jesus' instruction to "store up" treasures in heaven tells us we have the capacity to make deposits into a heavenly bank account. If this is true, could we also receive withdrawals from that account? Consider the story of Cornelius:

Now there was a man at Caesarea named Cornelius, a centurion of what was called the Italian cohort, a devout man and one who feared God with all his household, and gave many alms to the Jewish people and prayed to God continually. About the ninth hour of the day he clearly saw in a vision an angel of God who had just come in and said to him, "Cornelius!" And fixing his gaze on him and being much alarmed, he said, "What is it, Lord?" And he said to him, "Your prayers and alms have ascended as a memorial before God."

Acts 10:1–4

Cornelius "[lent] to the LORD" (Proverbs 19:17) by practicing almsgiving, one of the most ancient and secure investment strategies. When God sought a suitable candidate among the Gentiles to receive the blessing of salvation and the outpouring of the Holy Spirit, He chose a man whose heavenly bank account was mature. As Jesus taught, it is to those who have that more will be given (see Matthew 25:29).

In Scripture we learn of the principle of Jubilee, the cancellation of debt. Cancellation of debt is actually a dimension of the grace we receive through the cross, for the cross was itself the cancellation of our debt. We also learn of the principle of the locust's restitution, of God redeeming time and multiplying back to us all that has been killed, stolen or destroyed by the enemy. We learn the principle of giving for the purpose of honoring rather than only to meet needs. This list goes on, of course, and I urge you to study these principles for yourself under the guidance of the Holy Spirit.

Scripture holds keys to every aspect of wisdom we need to fulfill our purpose in God as prosperous souls and supernatural stewards. However, I also believe the Body of Christ has not fully tapped in to the power of walking in these ancient paths because we have not fully embraced our divine purpose. The pursuit of wisdom grows out of identifying and embracing what we were created to become and do. Until we perceive our destiny to have dominion for the preservation of many lives, as Joseph did, we won't tap in to the power of the storehouse or other divine strategies for wealth.

Embracing and living in our divine purpose as prosperous souls and supernatural stewards is more art than science. As good artists do, we must learn to take the materials of life as they come to us—in all their messiness, emotions and vulnerability—and discover ways of creating beauty, hope, joy, love and friendship from them all. An artistic approach to life will necessarily take time and space for dreams, for conversation and communion, for creativity and experimentation, for rest and for fun. This approach will make room for all the activities that enable us to build and sustain our relationships with God and with people, which is what life is about. True heavenly wisdom can always be seen in believers who adopt this artistic approach to life.

A scientific, formulaic approach to life usually breaks down because of its tendency to create a controlled, sterile, compartmentalized environment in which we focus on parts at the expense of the whole, and facts at the expense of relationship. Our scientific culture largely militates against an artistic approach to life and obscures the priority of relationships, so it is unsurprising that many people miss out on the benefits that come from the artistic way. Living in the present culture requires us to exercise faith and make sacrifices in order to tune out the stress, anxiety, selfishness, cynicism and hopelessness around us. We must take time to identify the things that are truly the most valuable and most important, and courageously practice developing, protecting and giving away—stewarding—those things. I can assure you that identifying and embracing your divine purpose is the most vital, rewarding thing you could ever do in life. Without it, you're not truly living!

Part of mastering the art of living in your divine purpose is identifying the realms of influence to which God has called you. The dreams and desires He has laid up in the wood grain of your life's purpose correspond to an area of life in which those dreams and desires, when realized, will release the blessing of who you are in God to those around you. This area could be a family, a church, a city or a nation. Or, it could be one of the realms of culture—business, government, arts and entertainment and so on. In whatever area to which you are called, there are people whom God has appointed you to bless. There are problems that God has appointed you to solve. He has promised that all of heaven will be at your disposal in fulfilling these appointments. He is simply waiting for you to seek Him for the wisdom to understand His heavenly purposes for your sphere of influence and to unlock the blessings and solutions He wants you to steward.

Solomon eradicated poverty in Israel. Shouldn't we believe that supernatural stewards in partnership with the same Spirit of Wisdom can eradicate poverty in nations today? Jesus healed all who came to Him. Who is to say that supernatural stewards cannot establish divine health in a city, region or nation? Such transformation has happened in the past, and it will happen again. Will you rise to the challenge and become a catalyst to change the world? Will you handle power in Jesus' name and allow Him to expand whatever is in your heart? Then join me in this courageous prayer and become a prosperous soul.

Beloved, I pray that in all respects you may prosper and be in good health, just as your soul prospers.

3 John 2

Acknowledgments

To Dawna, who holds me when I need it most.

To Cory and Timothy, who teach me courage.

To the De Silvas, Babcocks, Peerys, Reeders and Carters, for being real.

To Alan, for being.

To David, Richard, Marc and Renee, for your faithfulness.

To the leadership of Bethel Church, for being authentic when no one is watching.

To Bethel Church, for believing the Bible.

To Pam, Don, Loren and Faith, for provoking me to action.

To Dann, Edward, Jerry, Andre, Don, Julia, Mike, Doug and Rick, for your astute and gentle "do-overs."

To Allison, for your great strength and devotion to the craft.

To Jesus, the Lover of my soul.

And to Yaks Koffee Shop, for the soft chair, free rent and decaf cappuccinos.

Notes

Chapter 1 Purpose

1. www.bethelsozo.com
2. More information and bookings are available on the web at www.beth elsozo.com, or by contacting Bethel Transformation Center in Redding, CA, at (530) 246-6000.

Chapter 2 Trouble with Money

1. http://georgewbush-whitehouse.archives.gov/news/releases/2008/11/20081115-1. html.
2. Heather Whipps, "The Long History of the 2008 Financial Mess," LiveScience's History column posted: 19 September 2008 02:09 pm ET.

Chapter 3 Spirit of Poverty

1. "Poor young rancher wins $334m jackpot," *The Sunday Times* (Singapore), section 1, June 7, 2009.
2. Charles Dickens, *A Christmas Carol* (New York: The Peter Pauper Press, 1955), 20.
3. *New Oxford American Dictionary*, CD-ROM, version 2.0.3, Apple Inc., s.v. "Beelzebub."
4. Bill Johnson, *Strengthen Yourself in the Lord* (Shippensburg, Pa.: Destiny Image Publishers, Inc., 2007), 121–22.
5. Francis Frangipane, *The Three Battlegrounds* (Cedar Rapids, Ia.: Arrow Publications, 1989), 171.

6. Robert L. Thomas, ed., *New American Standard Exhaustive Concordance of the Bible/Hebrew-Aramaic and Greek Dictionaries*, CD-ROM, version 2.4, Oaktree Software, 6119.

7. Ibid., 3478.

8. Ibid., 8280.

Chapter 4 Trust and Faith

1. Erik H. Erikson, *Childhood and Society* (New York: W.W. Norton & Company, Inc, 1963).

2. The crossing of Niagara Falls with a wheelbarrow is true. The acrobat was Jean Francois Gravelet, known as Charles Blondin, who first crossed Niagara Falls on a tightrope in 1859. He also did it with a wheelbarrow filled with rocks, then asked a reporter to sit in the barrow. The reporter declined. He also carried his manager over twice. (Special thanks to Edward Quicke for this historic reference.)

Chapter 5 Dreaming

1. Tim Butcher, *Blood River: A Journey to Africa's Broken Heart* (London: Chatto and Windus, 2008).

2. *New Oxford American Dictionary*, s.v. "toil."

3. Thomas Cahill, *The Gifts of the Jews: How a Tribe of Desert Nomads Changed the Way Everyone Thinks and Feels* (New York: Nan A. Talese/Anchor Books, 1998), 144.

Chapter 7 Spirit of Mammon

1. C. S. Lewis, *The Complete C. S. Lewis Signature Classics* (New York: HarperCollins, 2002), 150.

2. This common misunderstanding deserves one minor clarification: It is the love of money (not singularly money) that is the root of all sorts of evil (not all evil as some believe). See 1 Timothy 6:10.

3. Daniel H. Pink, *A Whole New Mind* (New York: Penguin, 2005), 218.

Chapter 8 Dominion

1. Claude Hickman, "Count Zinzendorf," http://www.thetravelingteam.org/node/177.

Stephen K. De Silva is the chief financial officer of Bethel Church in Redding, California. As a certified public accountant since 1989, Stephen has worked in both public and private practice, with specialties in small business consulting, personal finances and administration for non-profit organizations. His unique voice on stewardship and money is featured in the financial deliverance ministry Prosperous Soul. Stephen enjoys life with his wife, Dawna De Silva, founder and co-leader of the international healing and deliverance ministry Bethel Sozo.

For more information on the concepts in this book, consider Stephen De Silva's workbook, *Prosperous Soul Stewardship Series, Foundations Manual*, published by Accent Digital Publishing, Inc. (September 1, 2010), available online at www.prosperoussoul.com (Select the "Store" menu), or by calling Bethel Media at 530-351-7500, or by e-mailing customerservice@ibethel.org.

To order additional copies of this book at volume discounts, you can make your request in this same manner.

If you prefer, you can find audio and video content by Stephen De Silva at www.prosperoussoul.com. Select the "Store" menu.

If you are interested in attending a live seminar or school, contact us for information by e-mailing your request to prosperoussoul@ibethel.org.

If you are interested in running a Prosperous Soul small group in your church or home, we suggest the full product line of Prosperous Soul Foundations (7-disc DVD or CD series) with volume discounts available for books and manuals at www.prosperoussoul.com.

If you would like to support our domestic and international efforts, contact us at prosperoussoul@ibethel.org.

Made in the USA
Lexington, KY
13 June 2014